Joseline Hernandez

Love & Hip Hop Diva

Marlow Martin

Joseline Hernandez   is an American-Latina rapper who is currently starring on the VH1 show Love & Hip Hop: Atlanta and has a net worth of $150,000. She was born in Puerto Rico in 1986 and moved from Puerto Rico to Miami at the age of 10. Joseline Hernandez is a young, up and coming rapper trying to catch a big break in the Atlanta music scene.

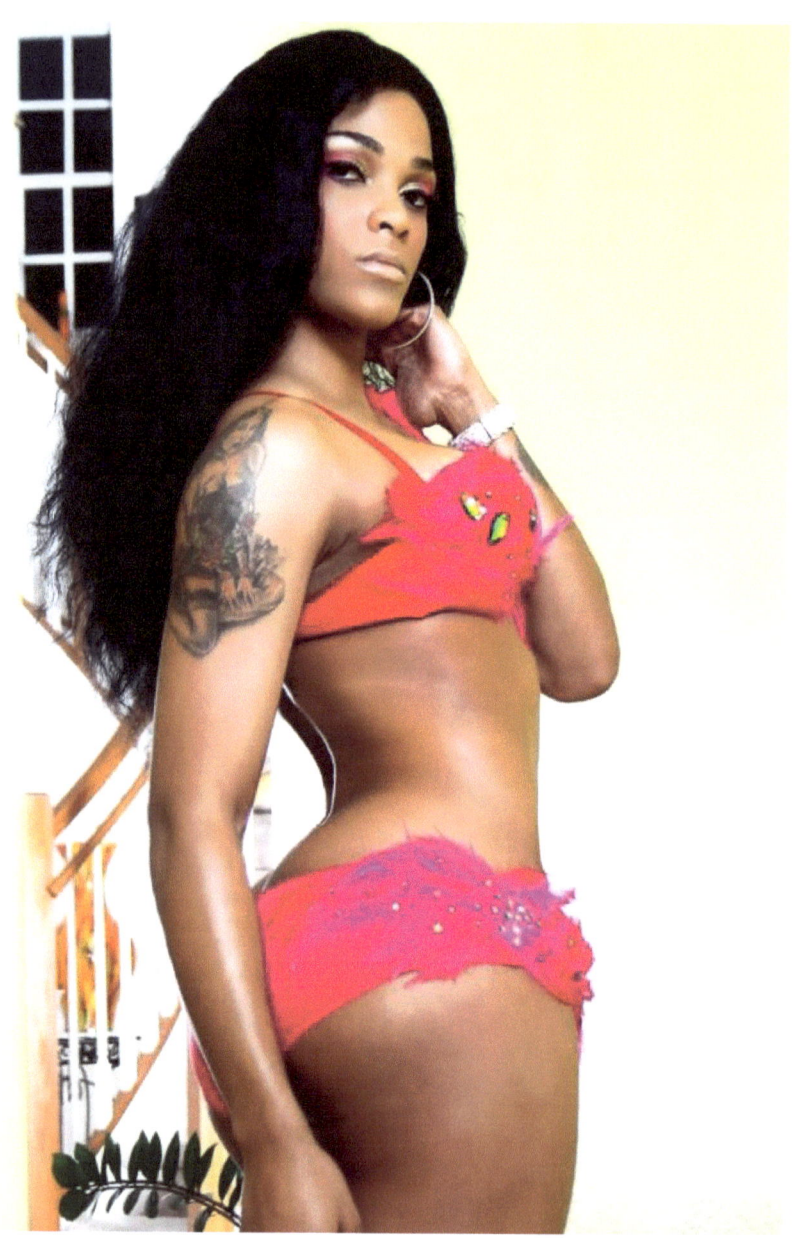

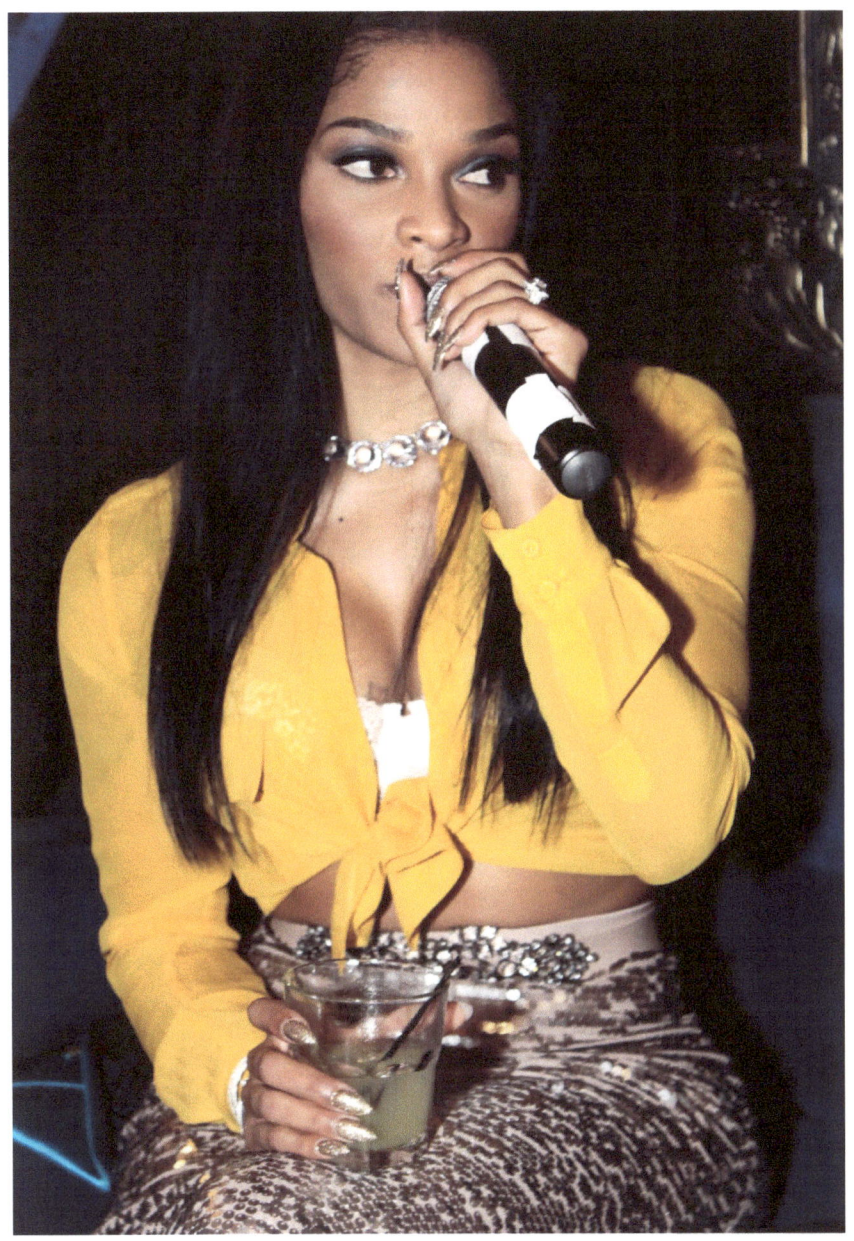

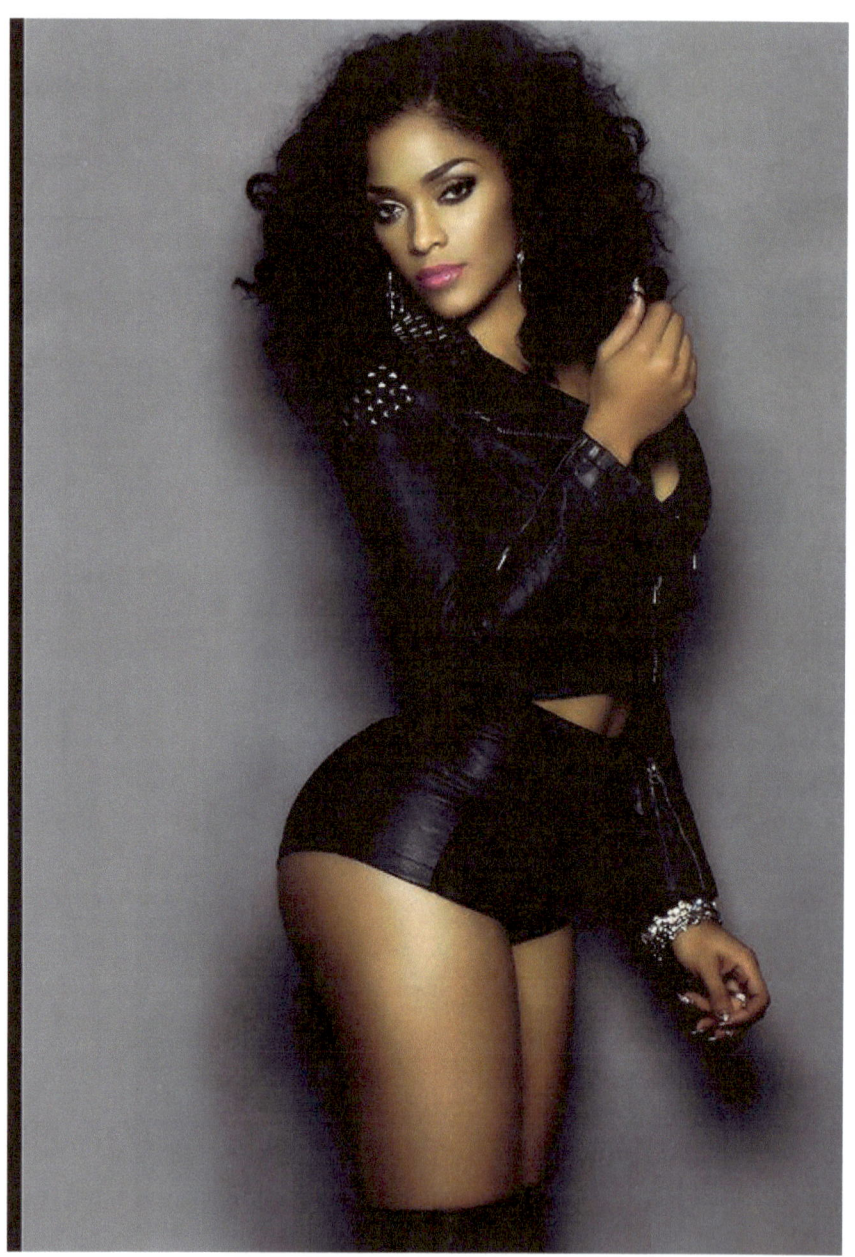

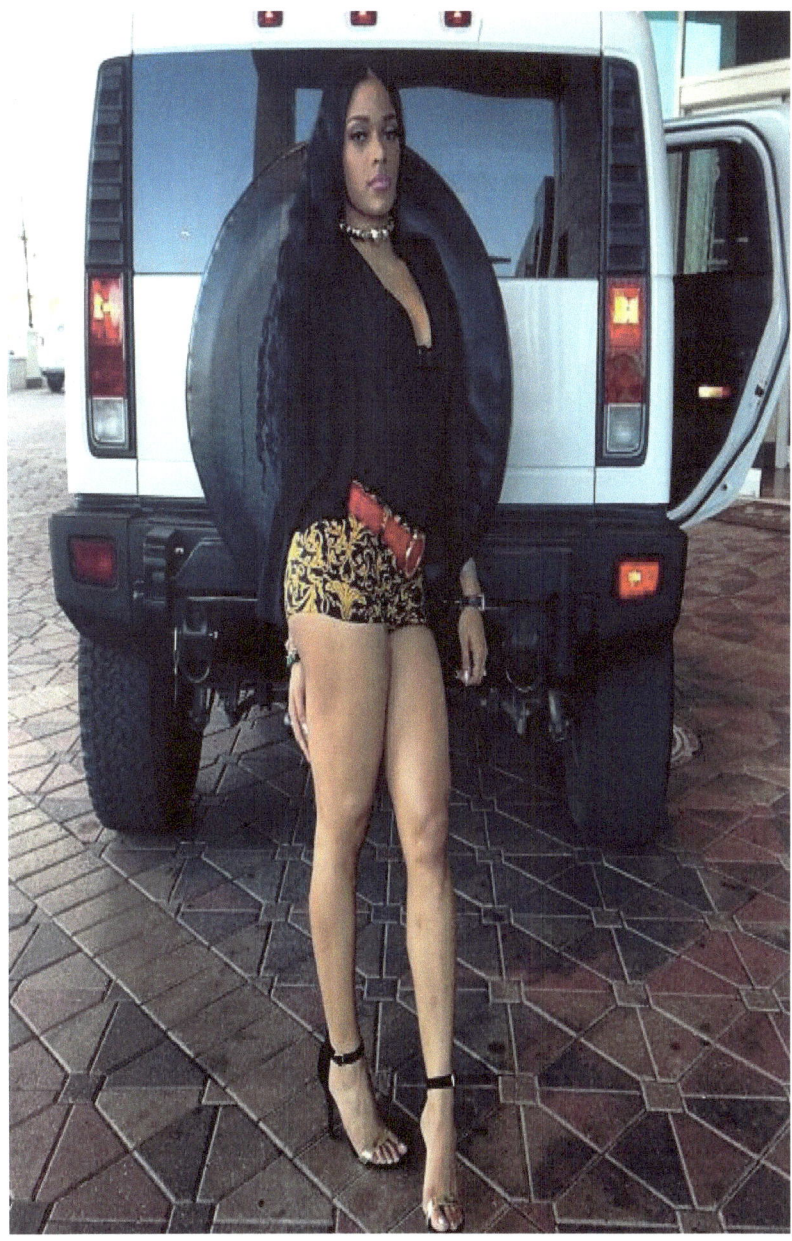

4

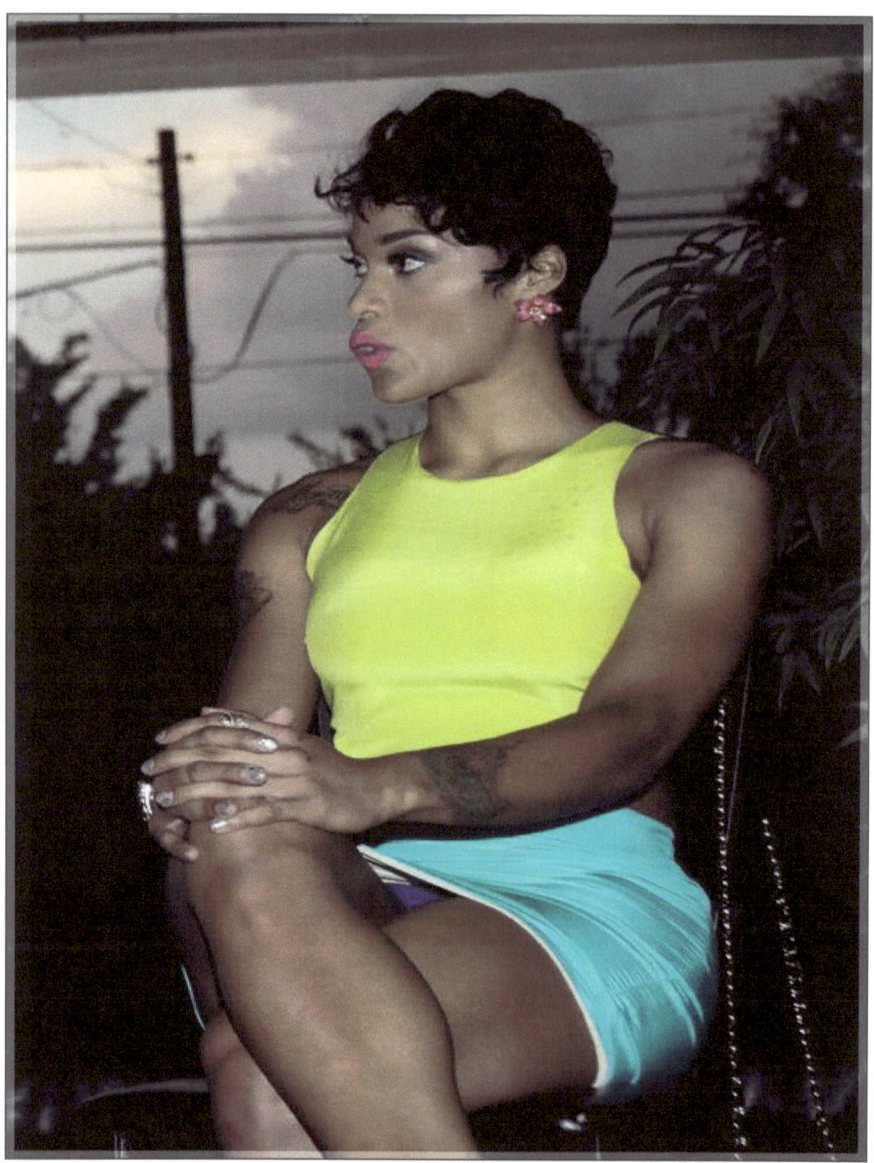

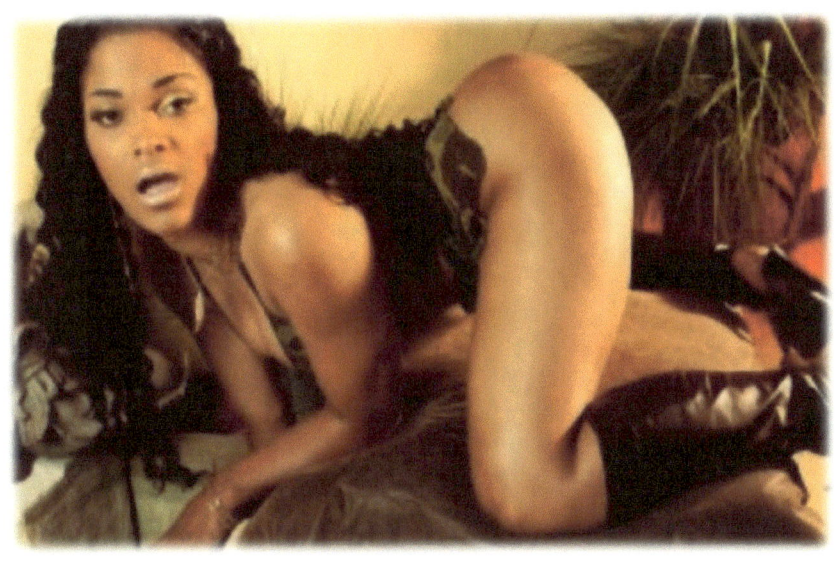

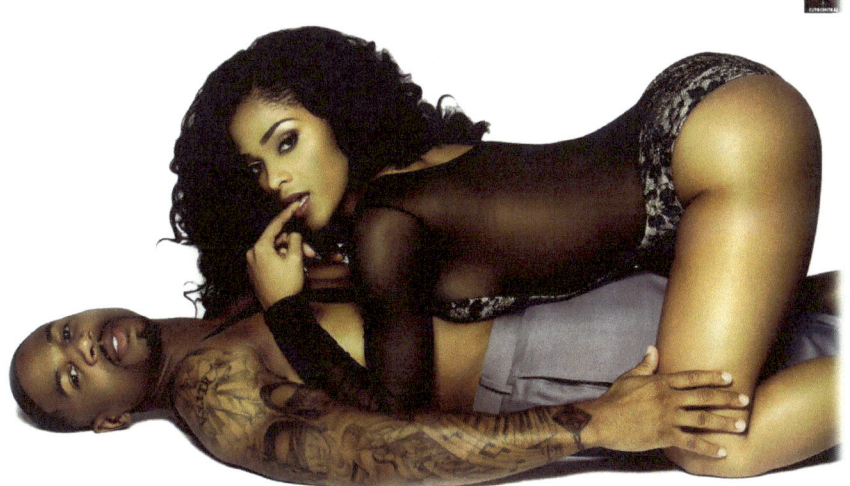

6

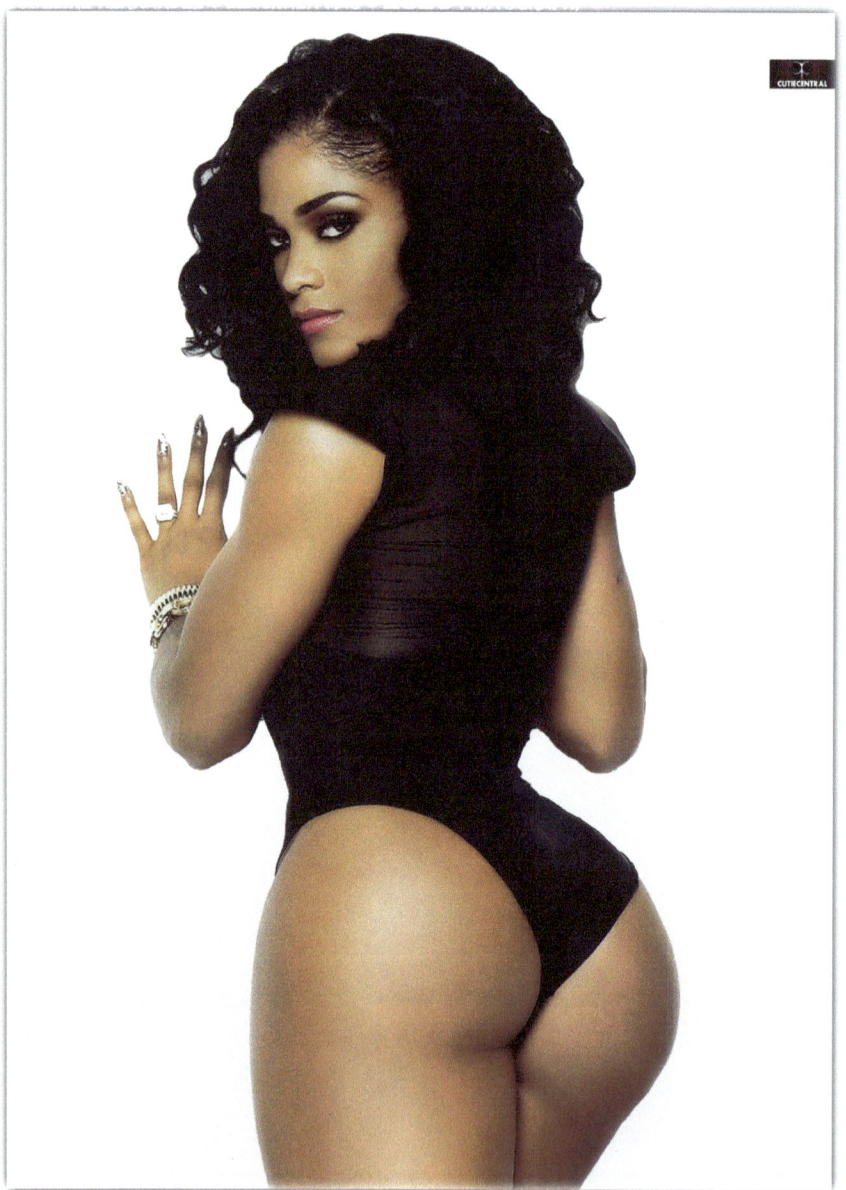

7

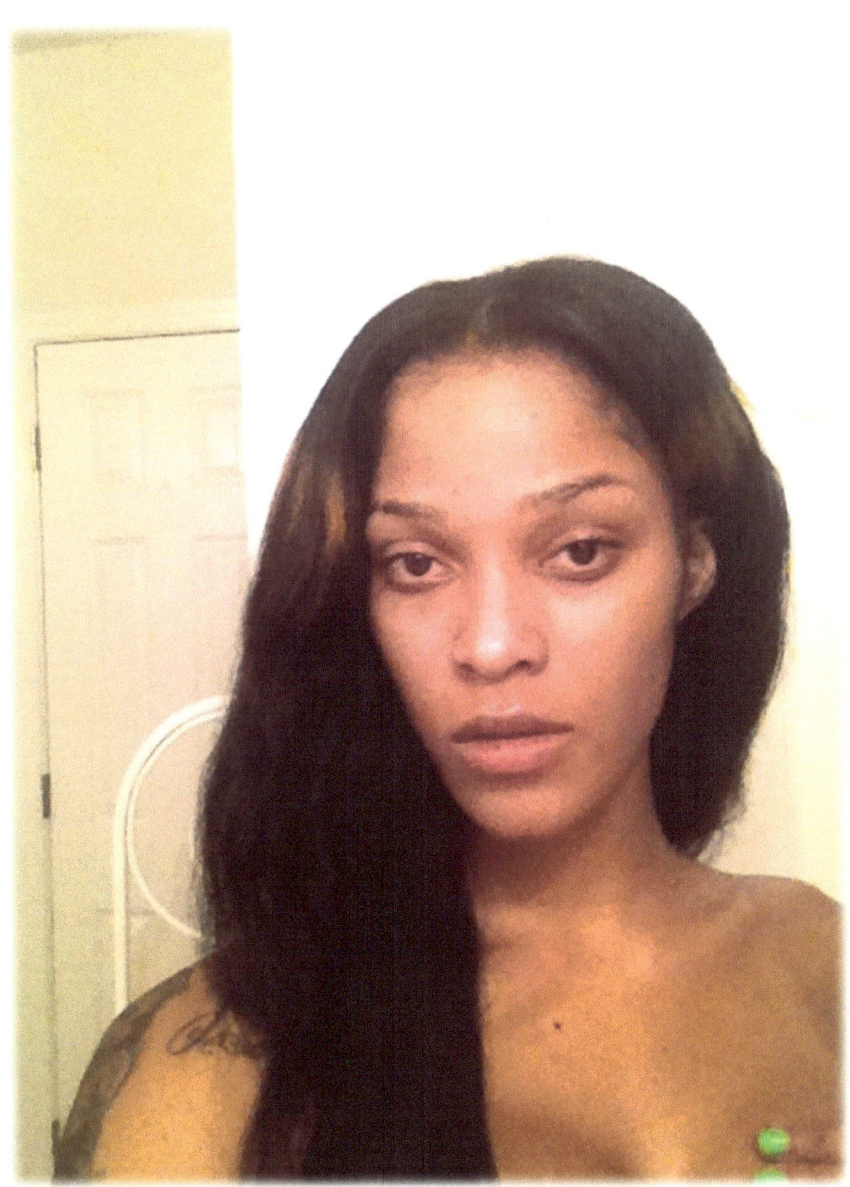

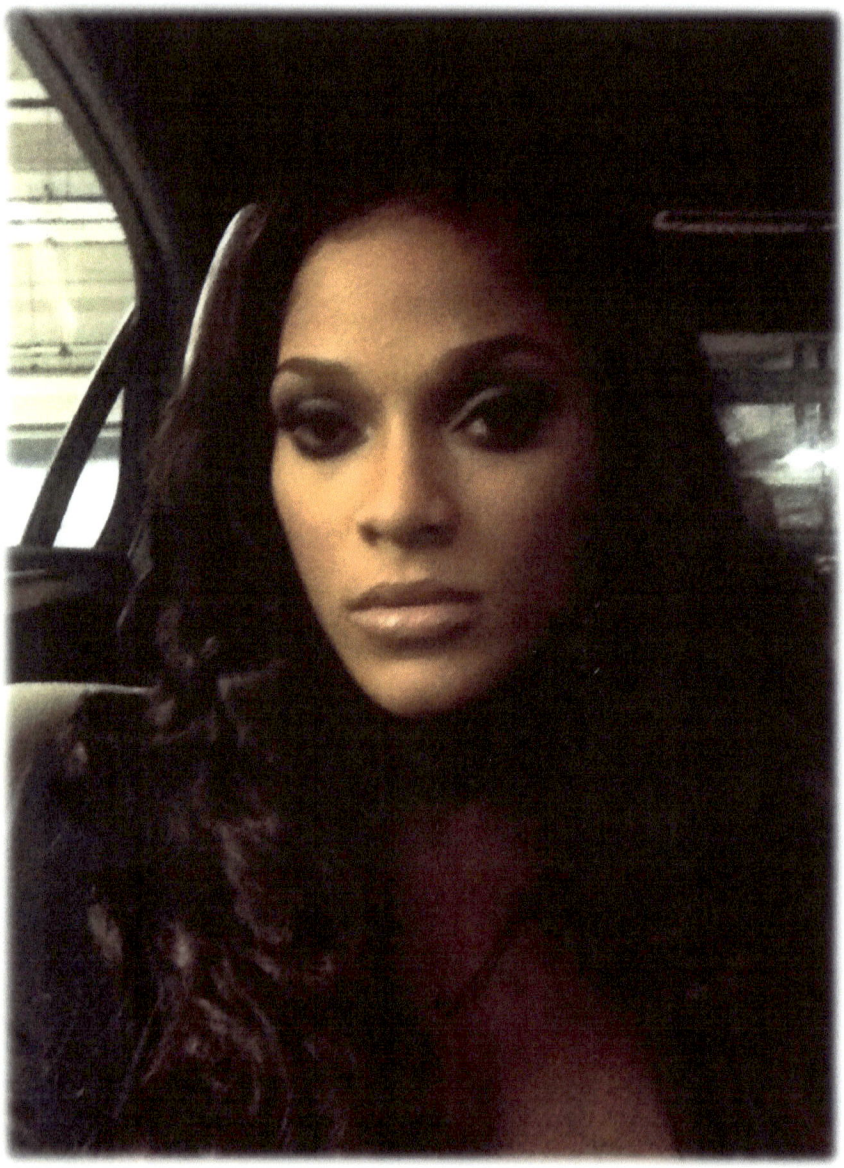

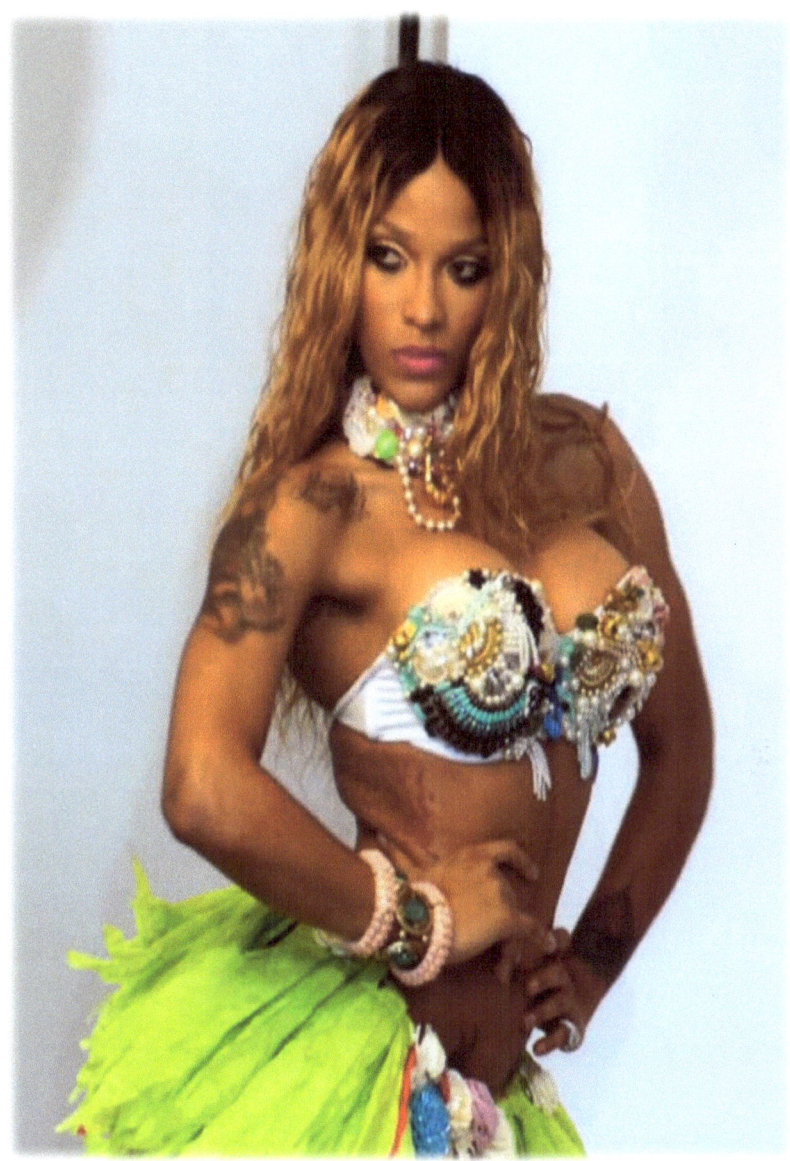

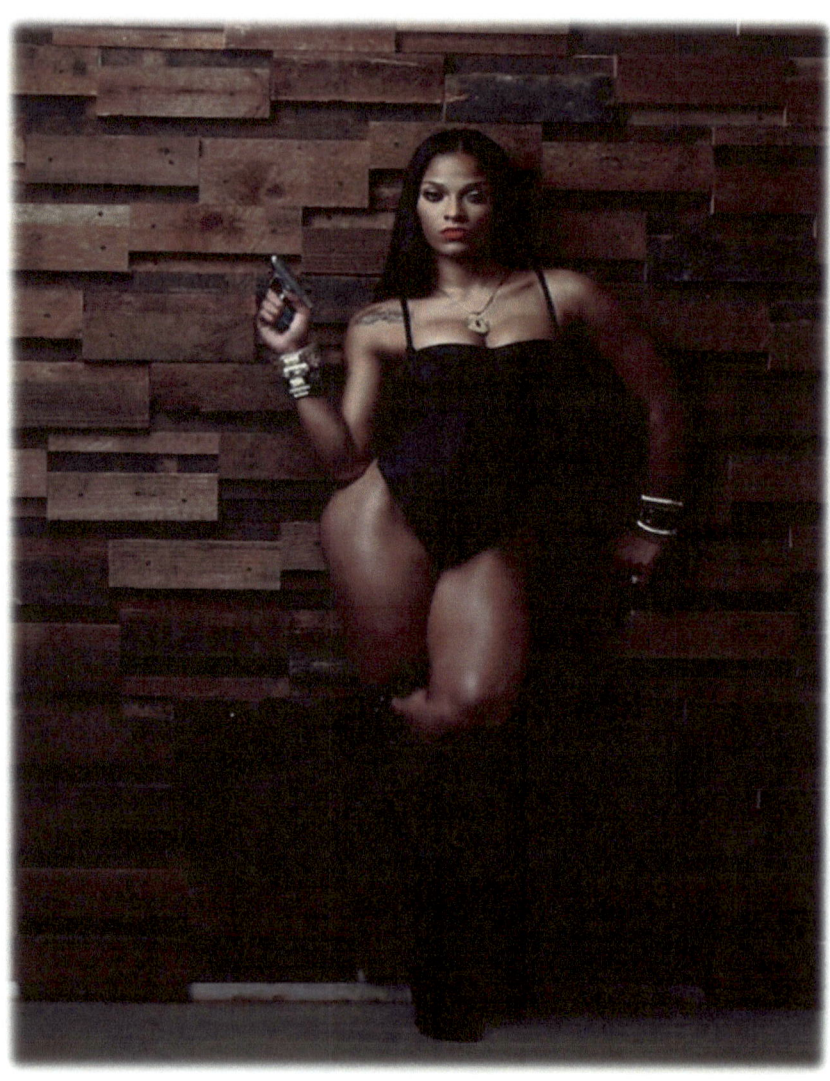

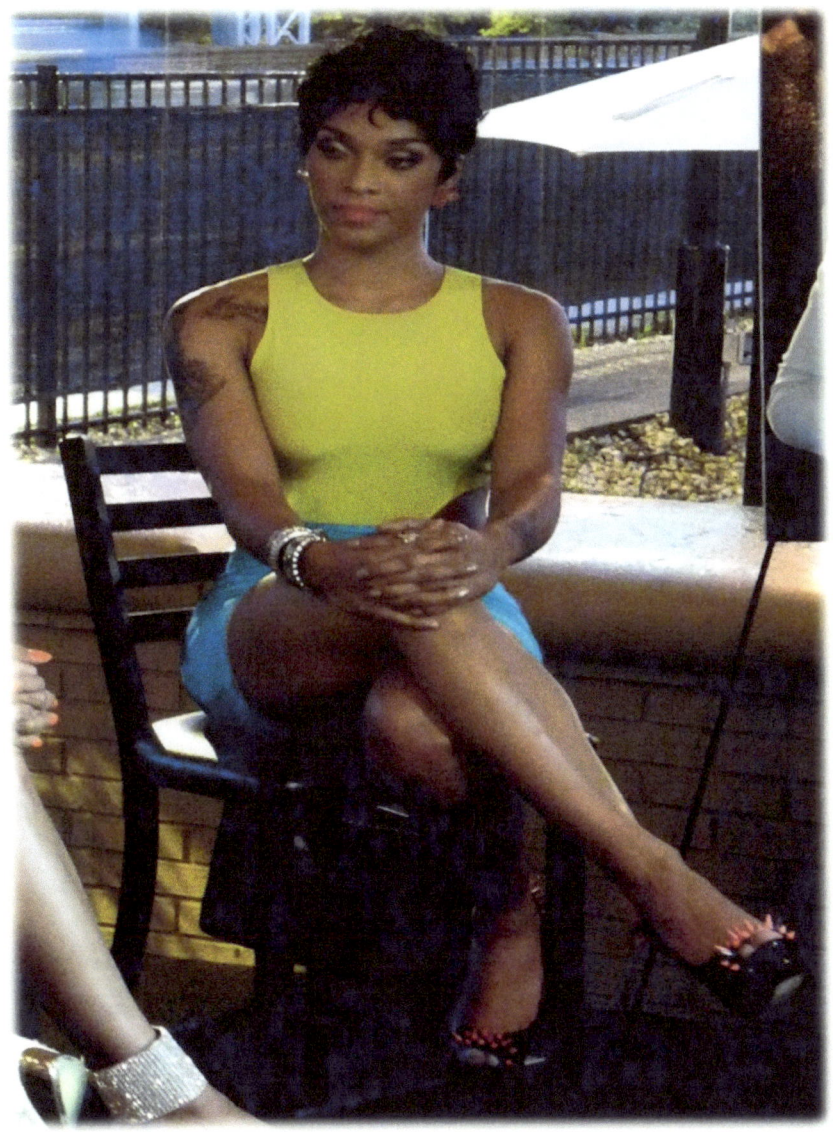

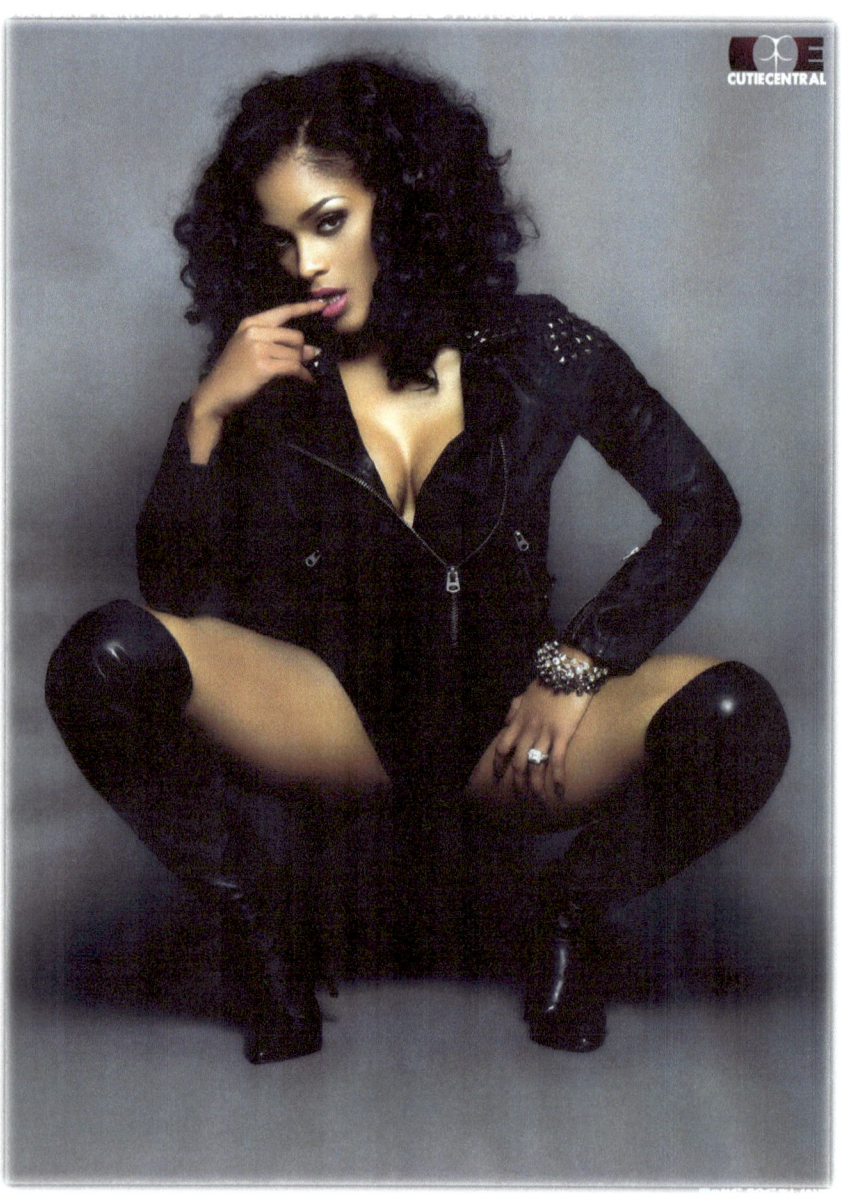

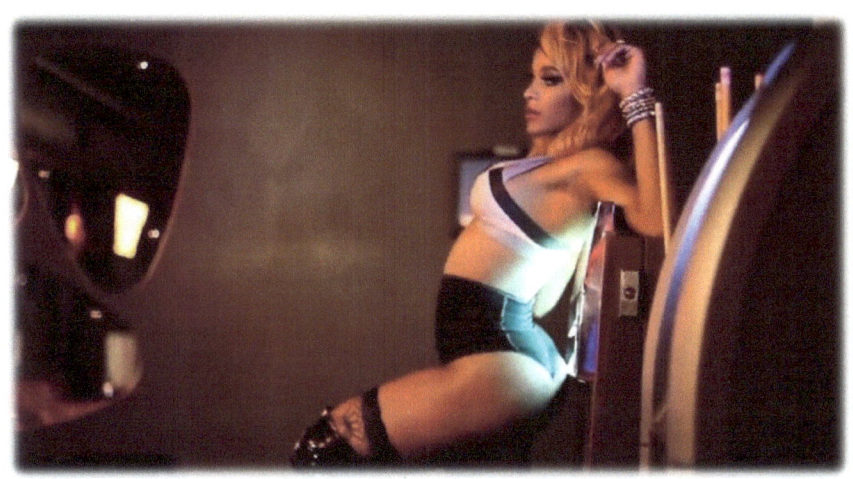

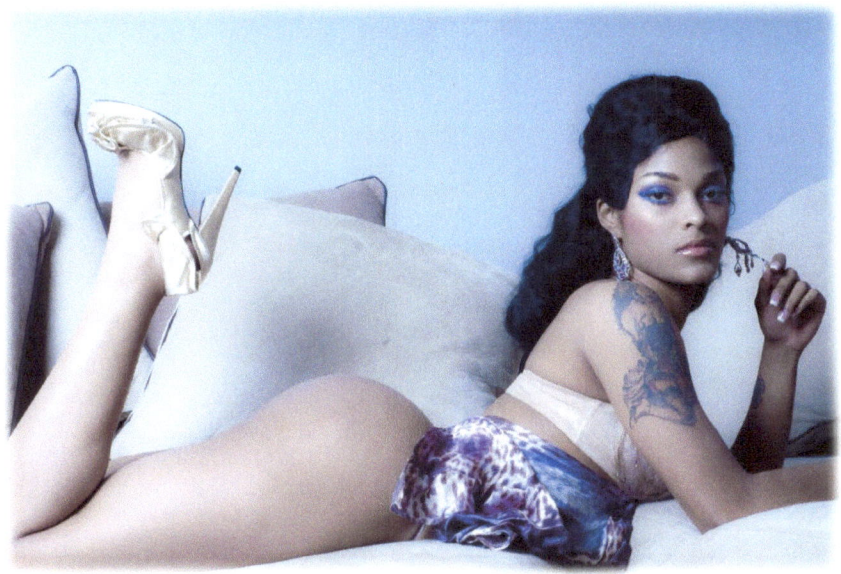

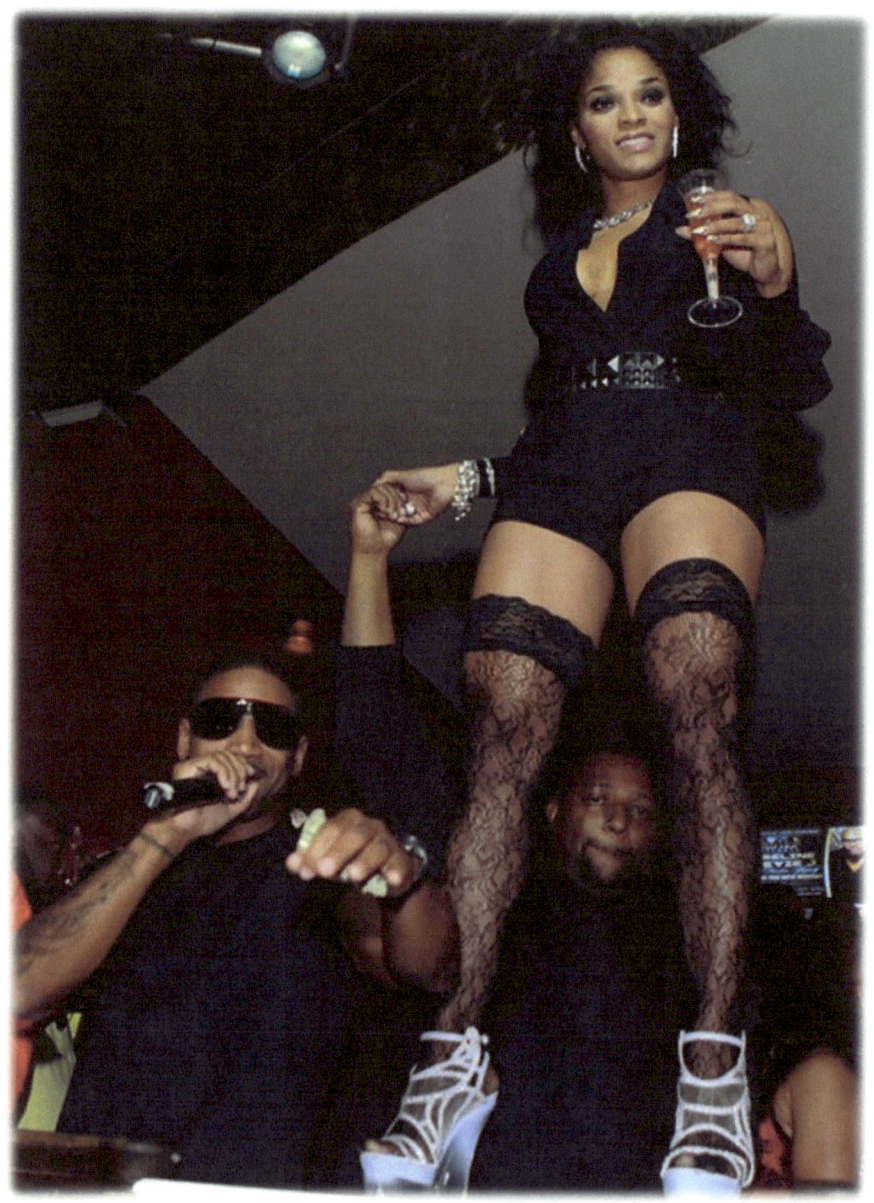

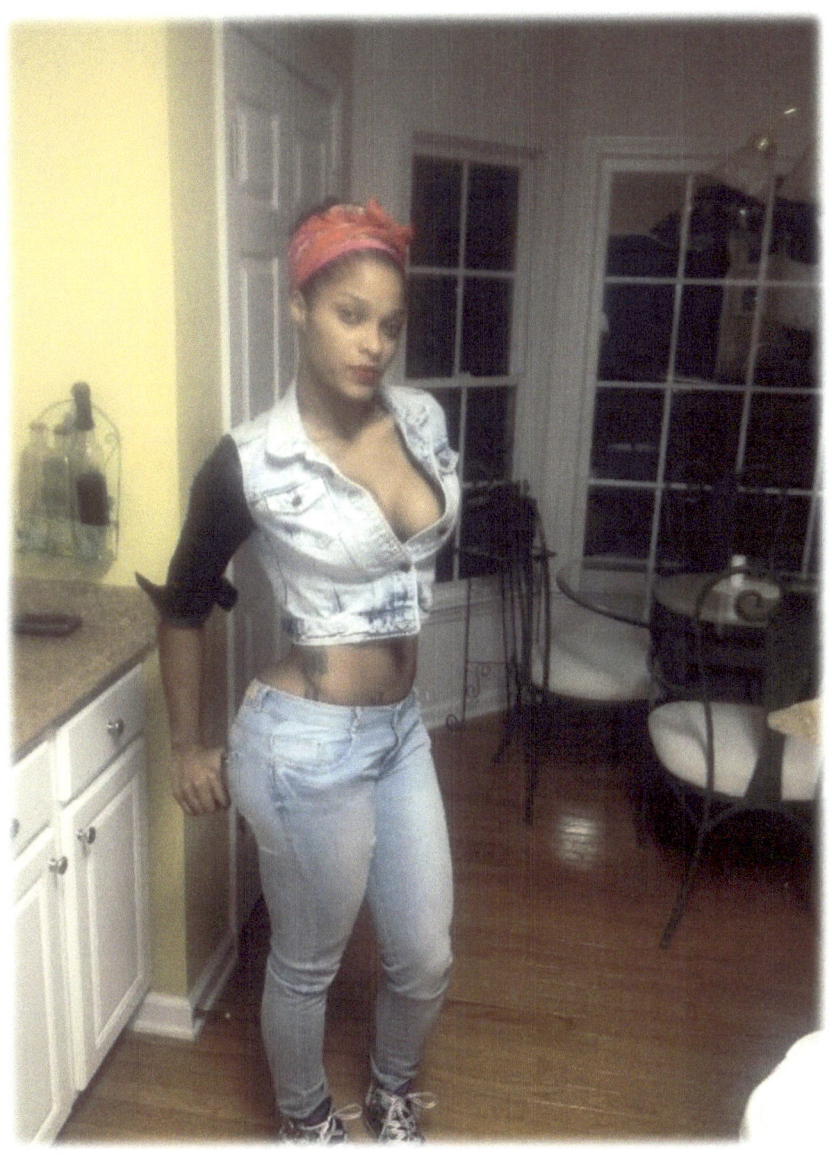

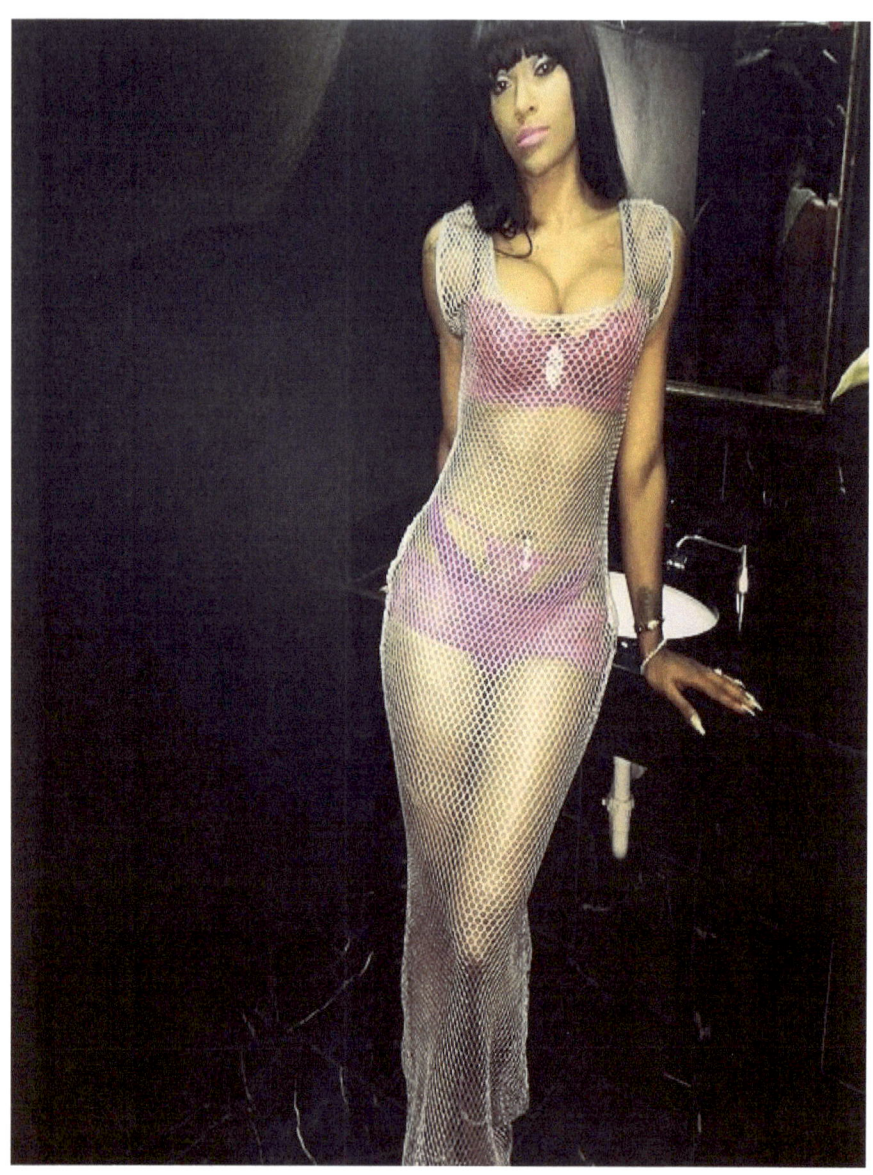

Joseline Hernandez *net worth: Joseline Hernandez is an American-Latina rapper who is currently starring on the VH1 show Love & Hip Hop: Atlanta and has a net worth of $150,000. She was born in Puerto Rico in 1986 and moved from Puerto Rico to Miami at the age of 10.*

Joseline Hernandez is a young, up and coming rapper trying to catch a big break in the Atlanta music scene. Before getting into rap, Joseline Hernandez was a stripper but eventually left dancing to follow her dreams. .

At one time, she performed as Shenellica Bettencourt and under that name, she was arrested for "lewd and lascivious behavior" in 2003. Hernandez claims she started stripping to help her family who were struggling financially. She has five brothers and sisters and one of her brother's has autism, so she used the money she made stripping to help pay for the mortgage, food, and medical bills for her family.

She is now beginning to make a name for herself in the music industry and is managed by Stevie J who is also her husband and fellow co-stars on Love & Hip Hop: Atlanta. Her stripping past makes Joseline Hernandez an outcast on the show.

Many of the other women, including Mimi Faust, have criticized her in the past for performing as a stripper but the criticism is not a surprise considering Stevie J was once dating, and has a child with, Faust. Hernandez has been a member of the cast of Love and Hip Hop: Atlanta since season one, and her relationship with Stevie J has been documented throughout the show. But let's be real, Joseline is a bad young woman!!!

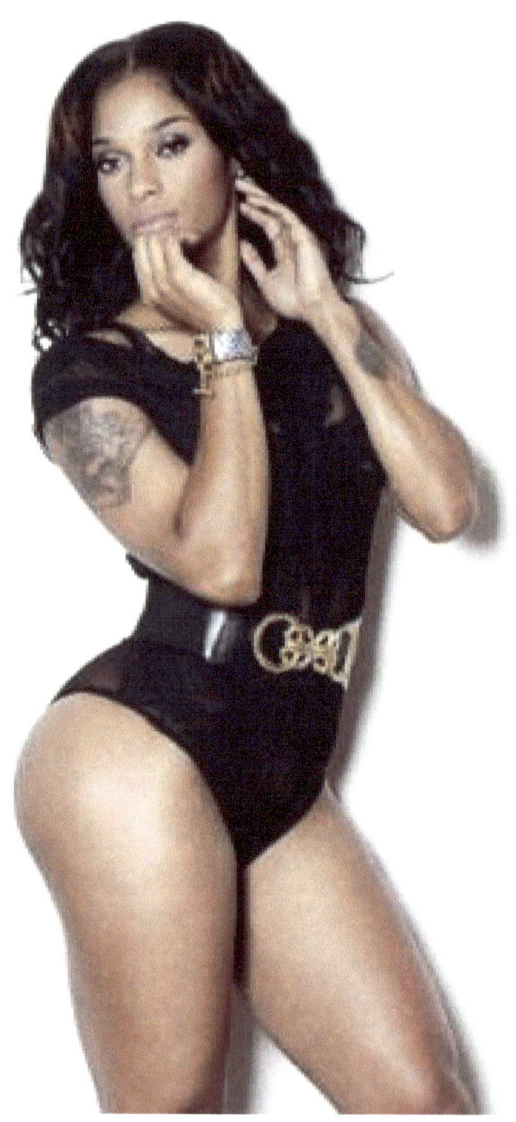

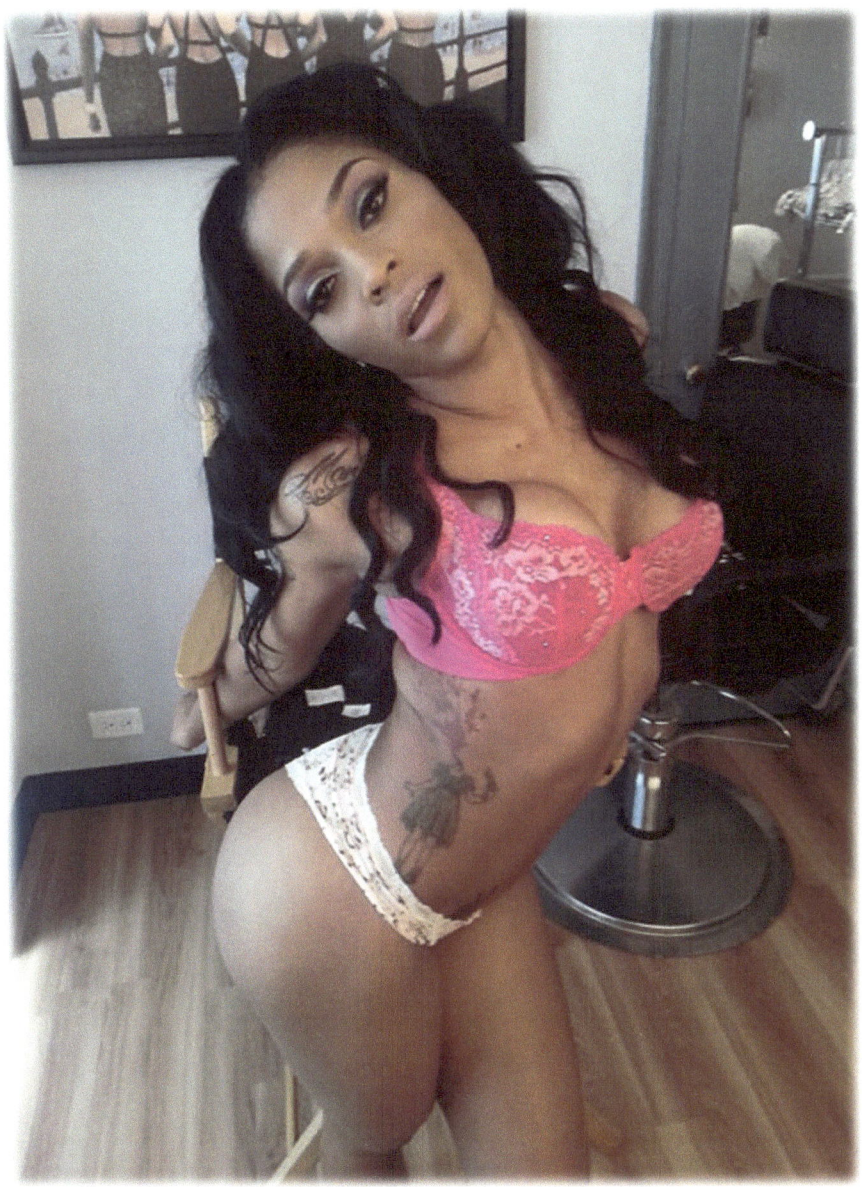

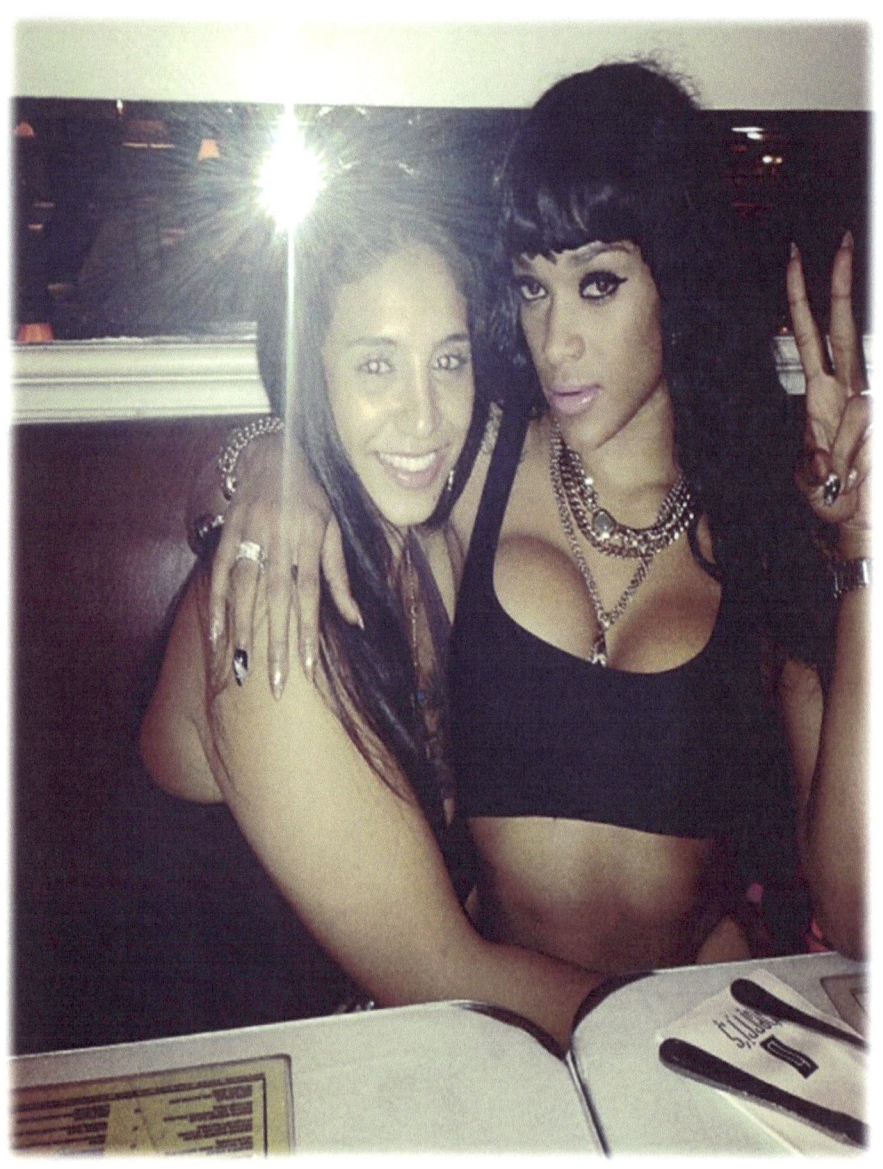

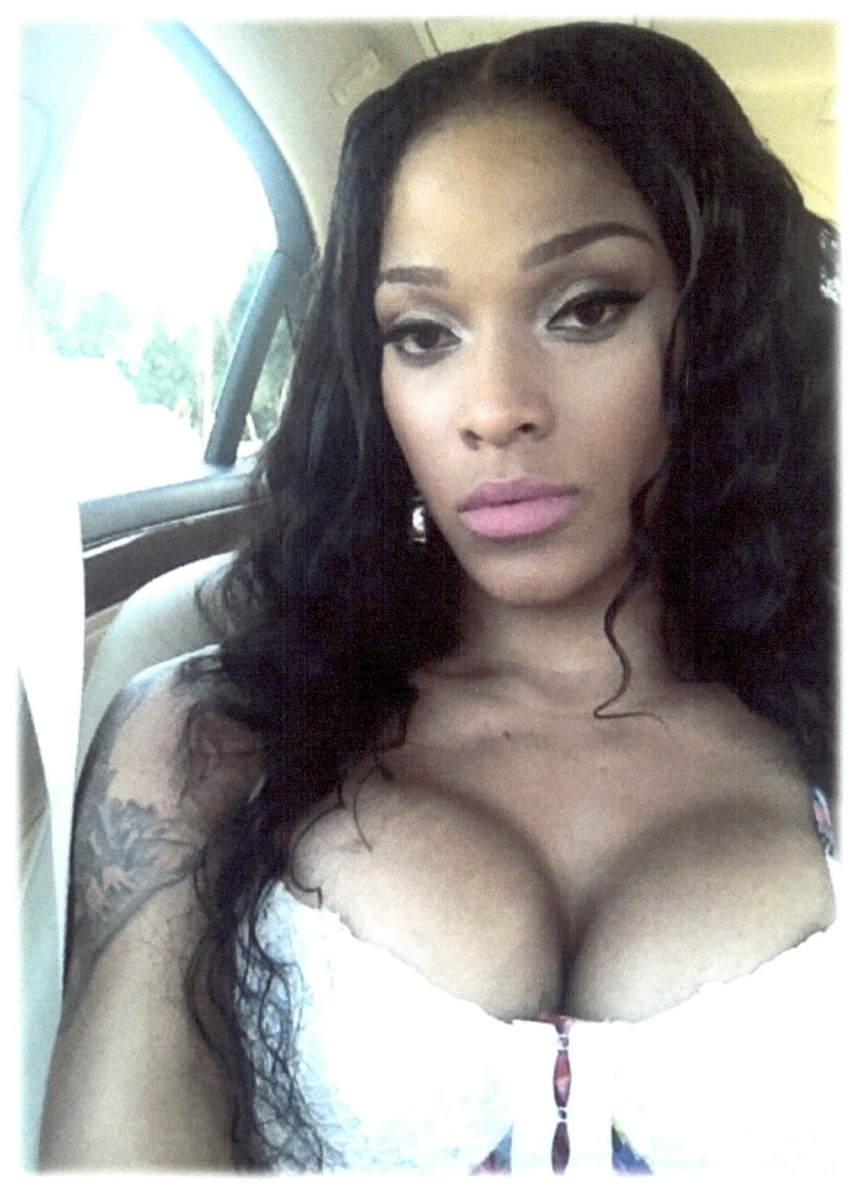

22

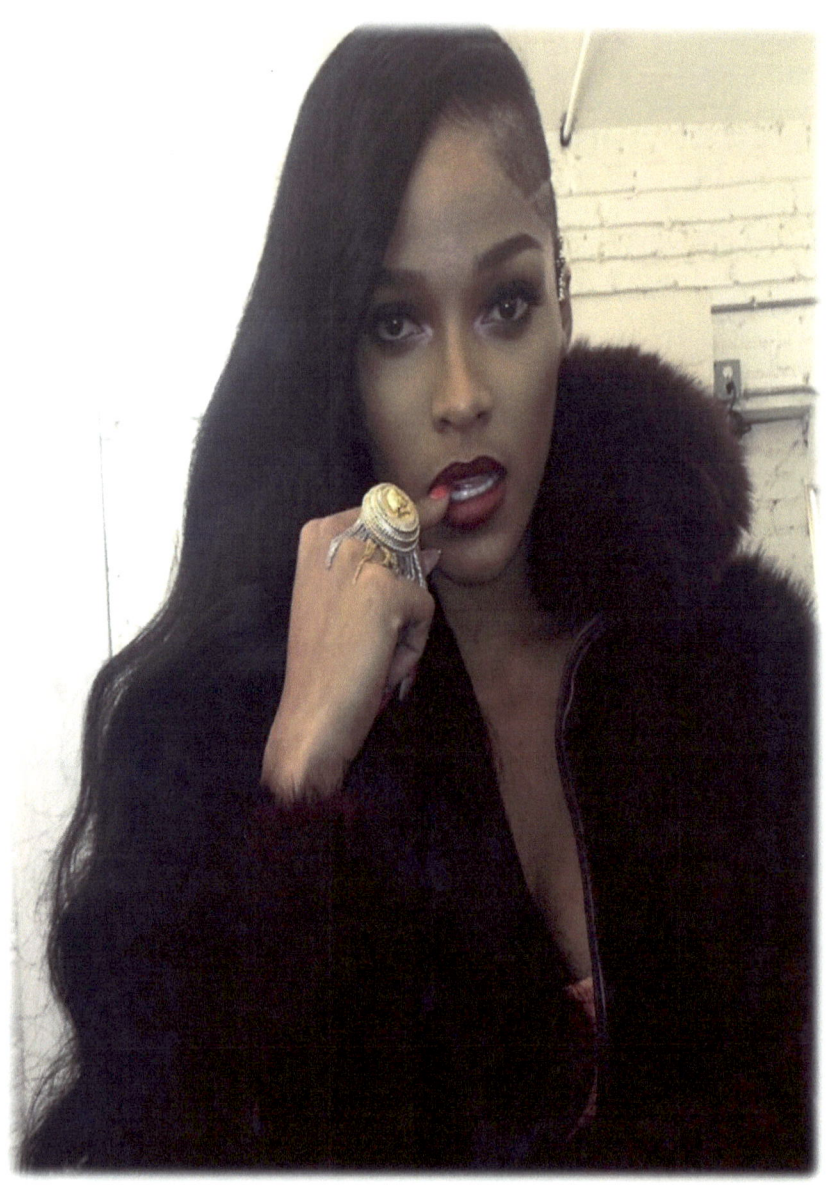

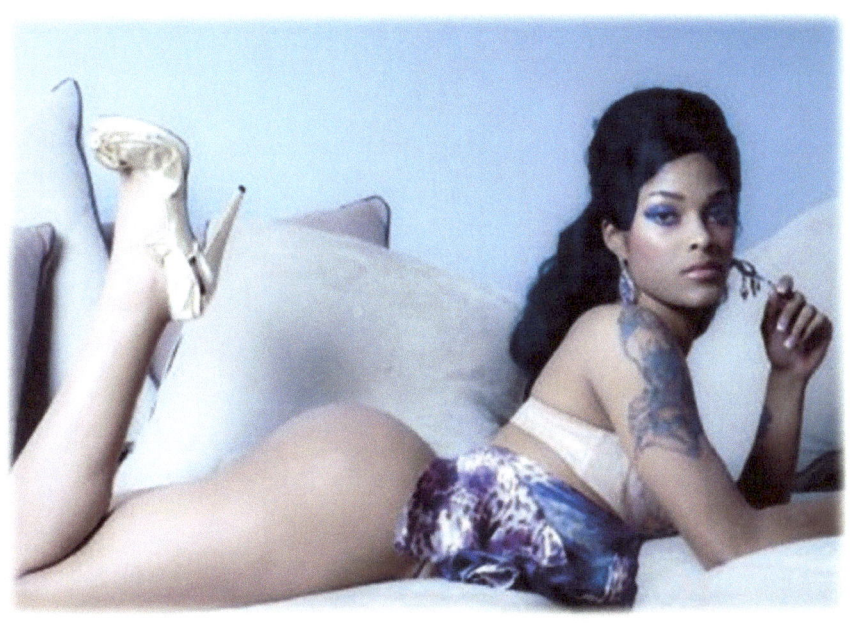

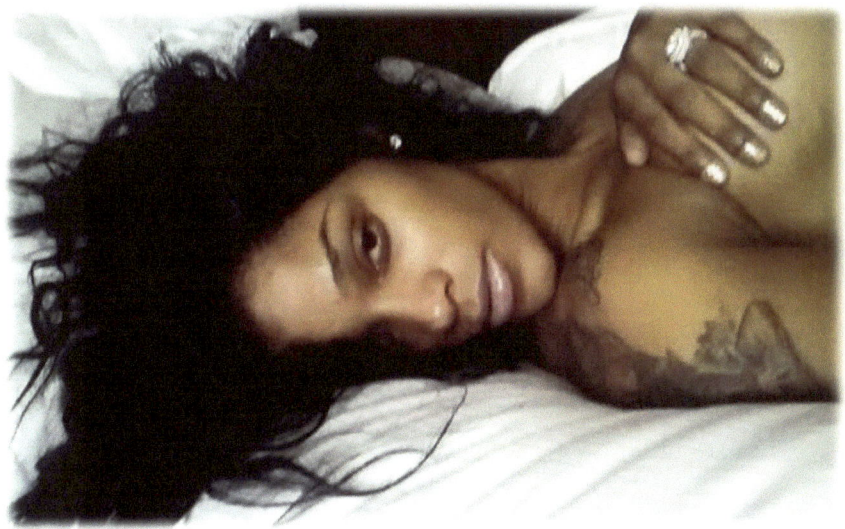

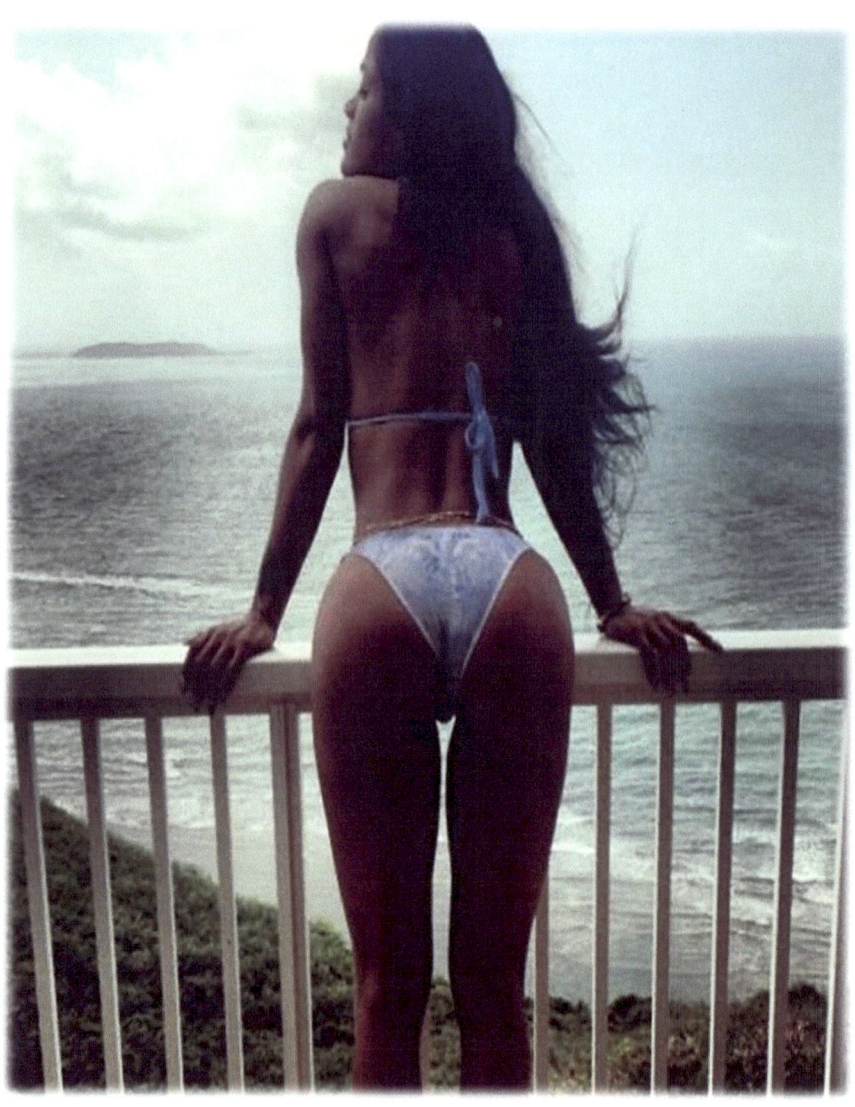

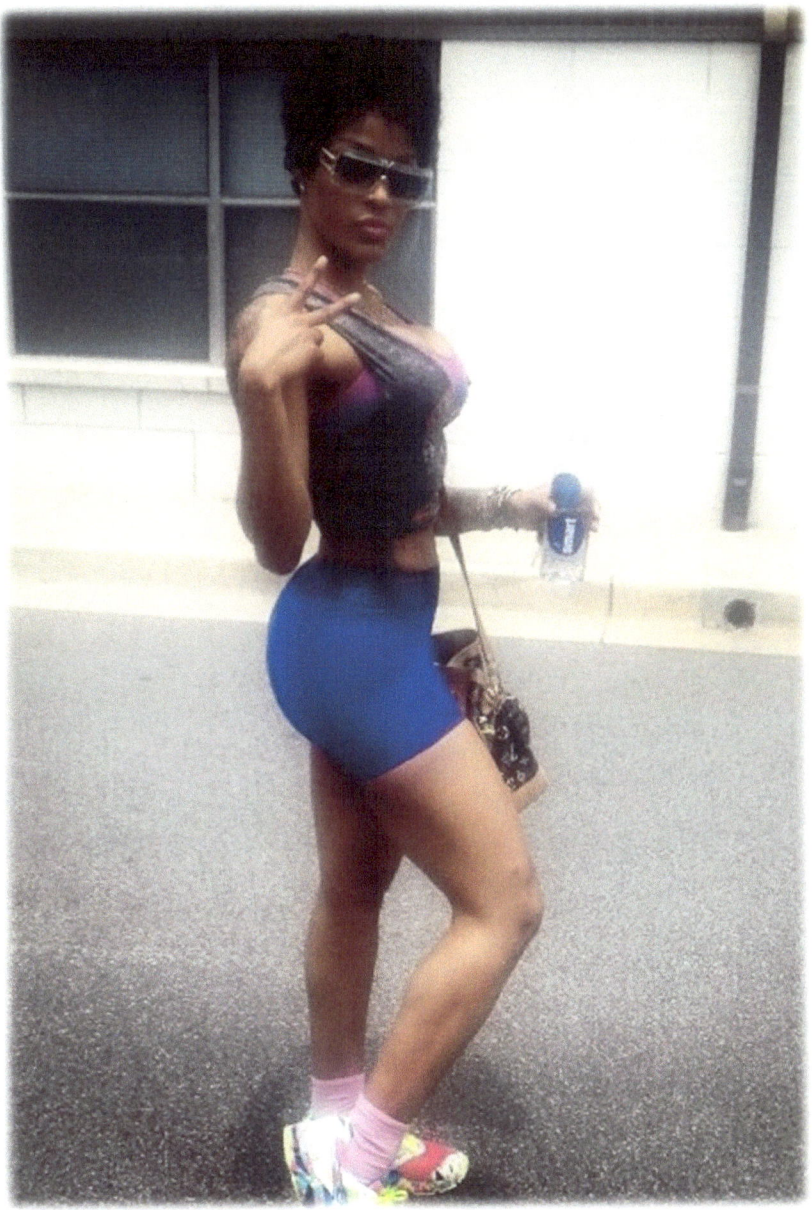

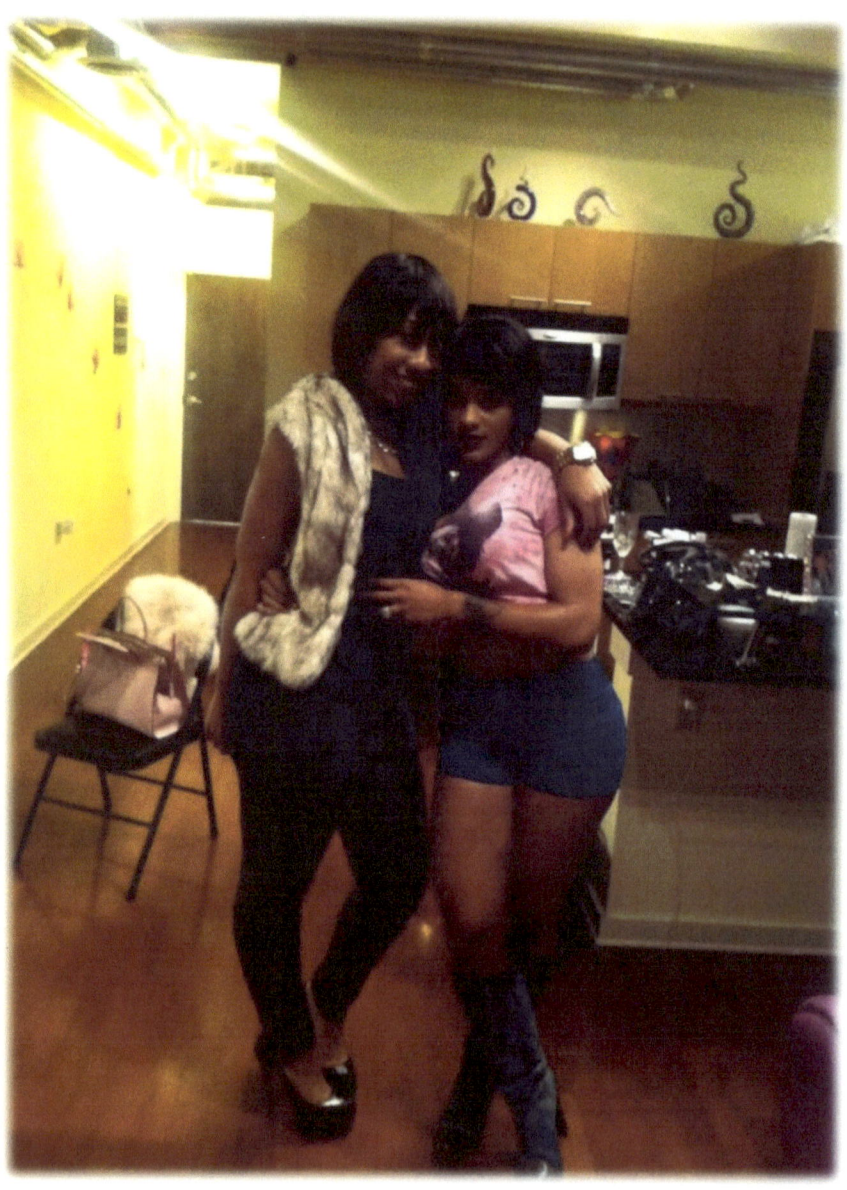

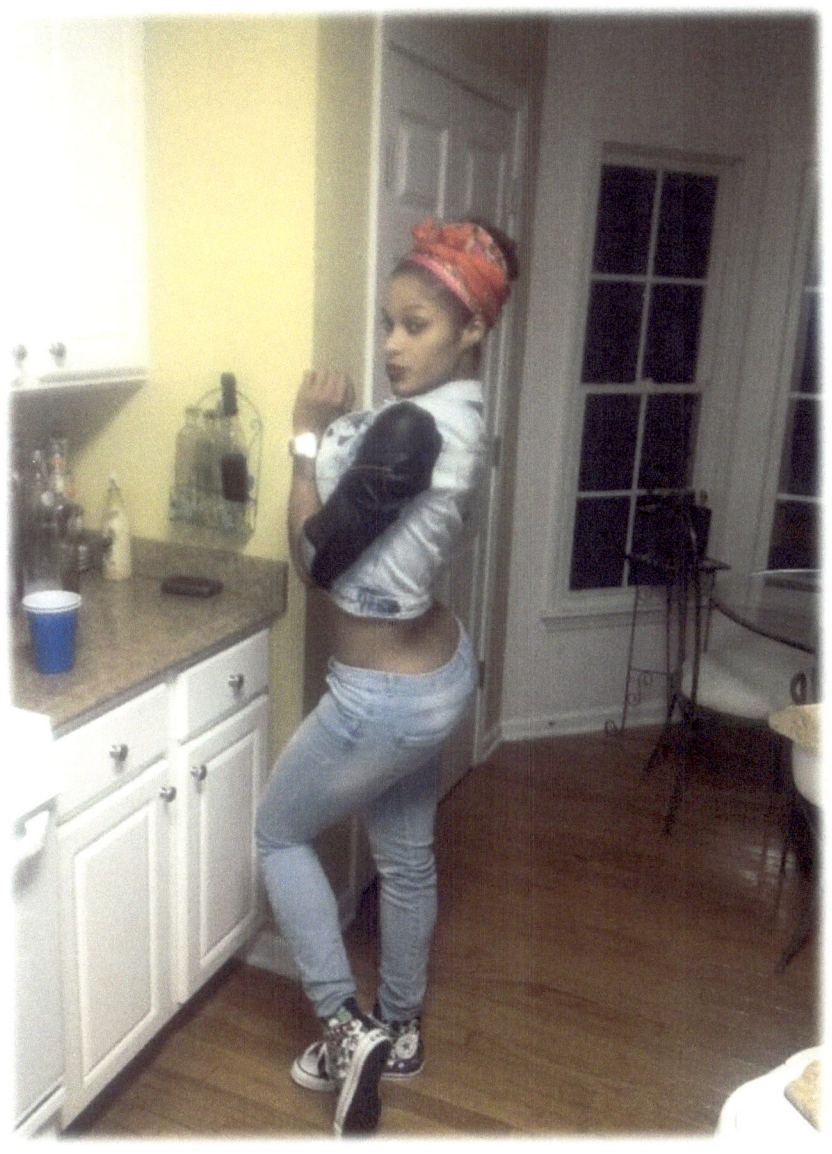

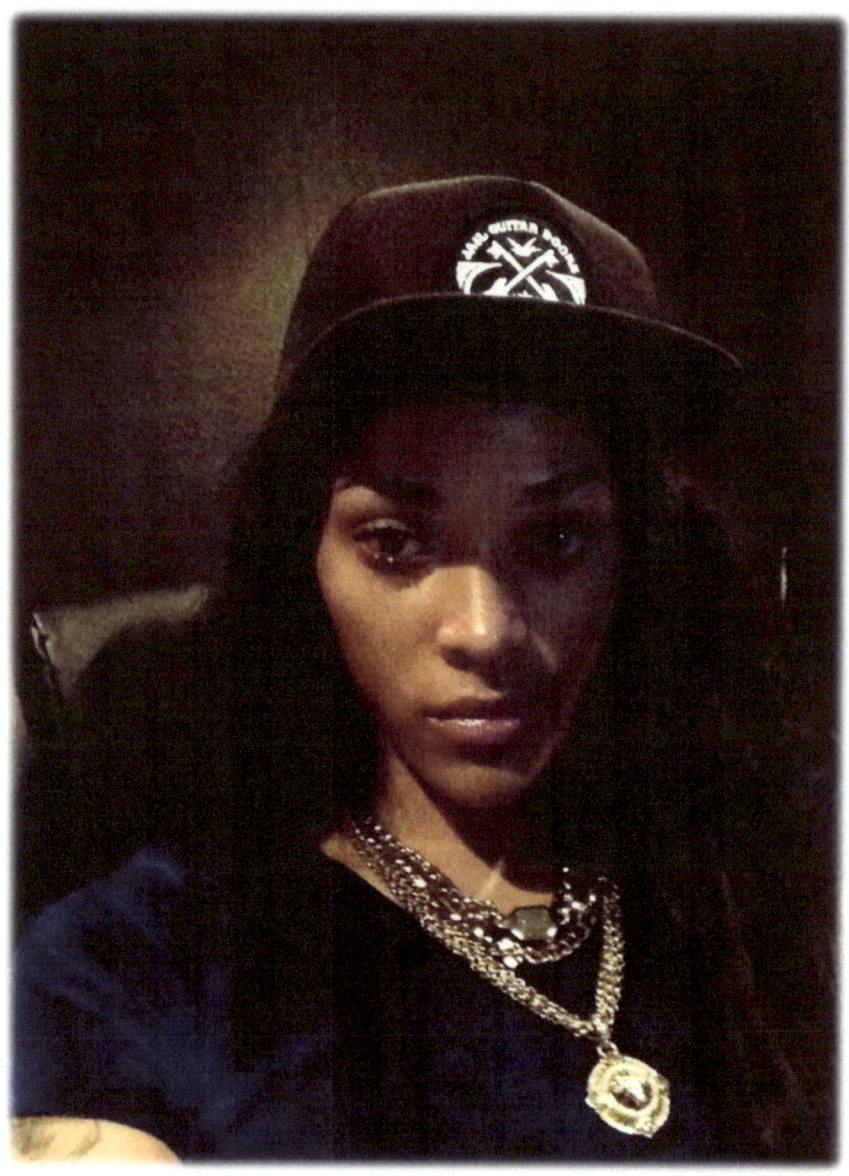

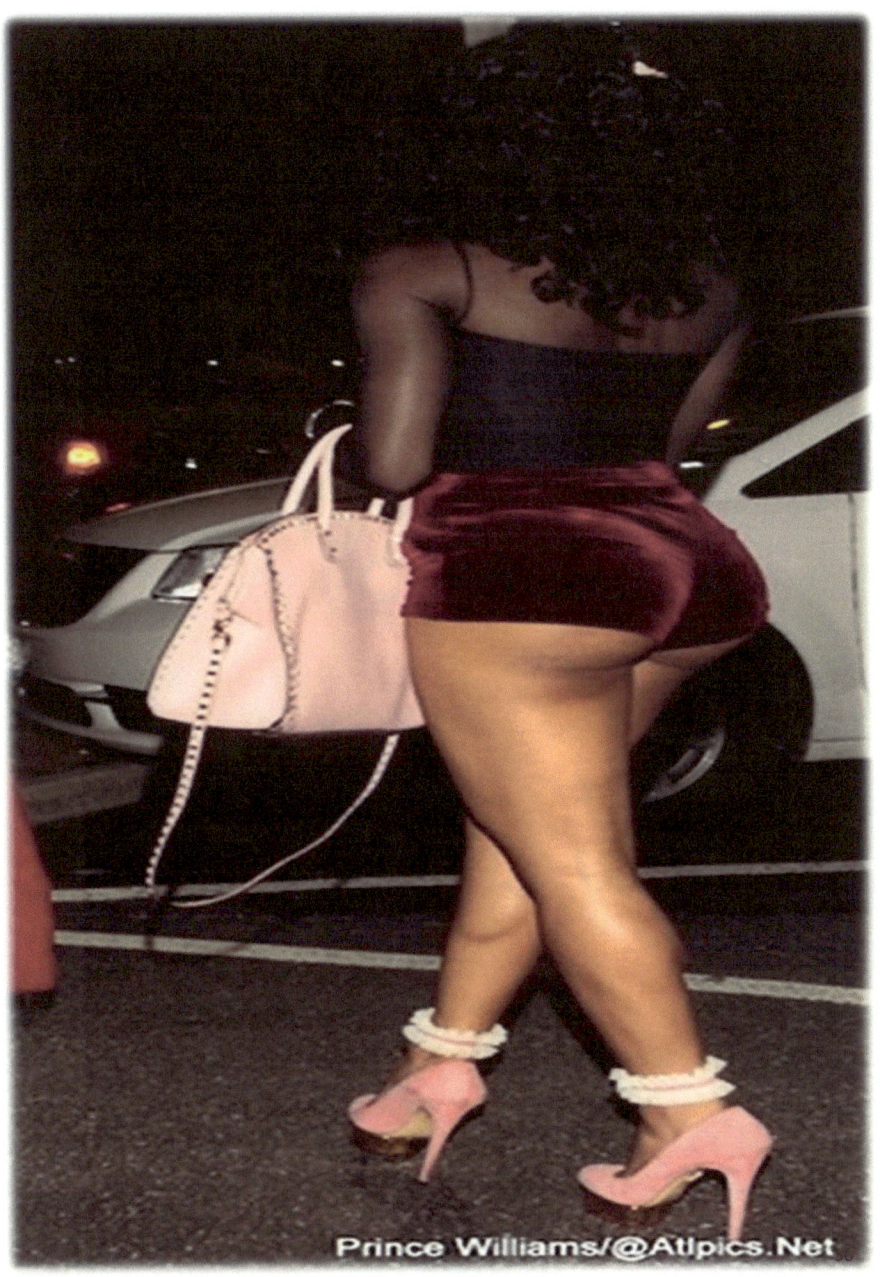

Prince Williams/@Atlpics.Net

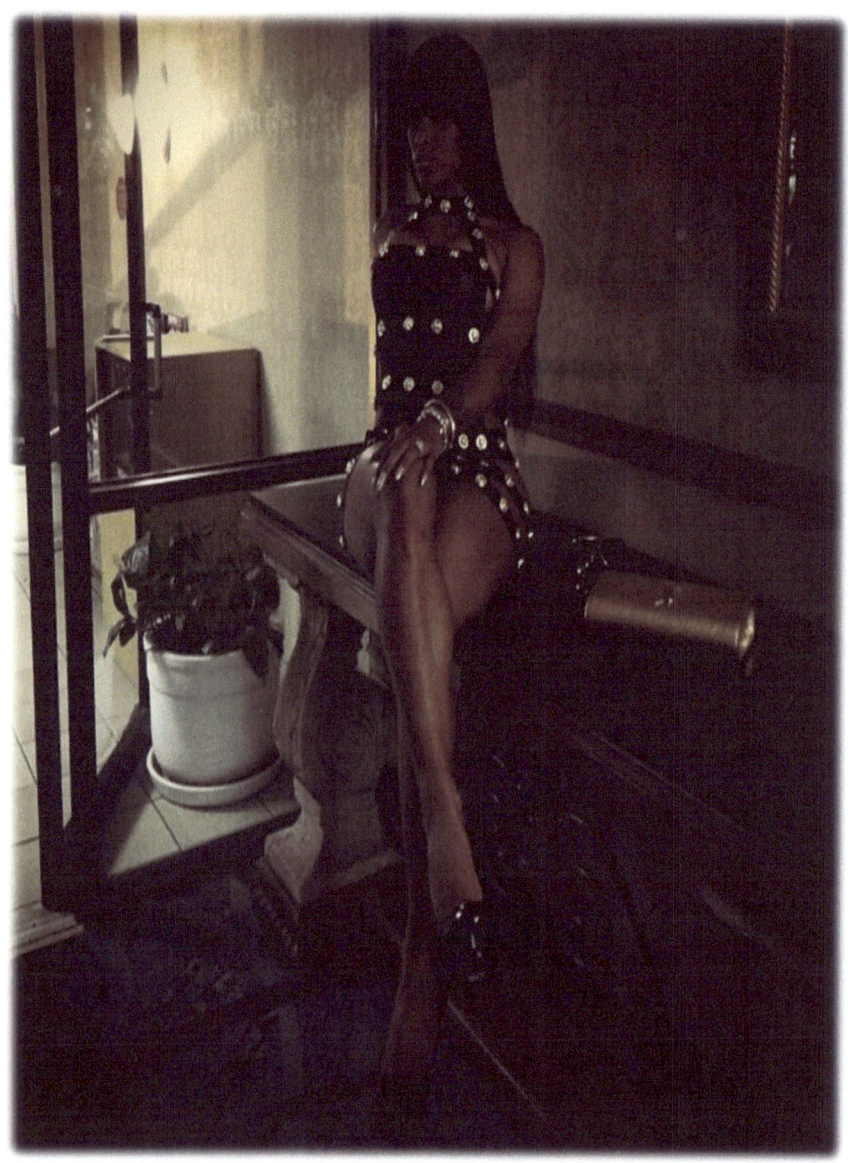

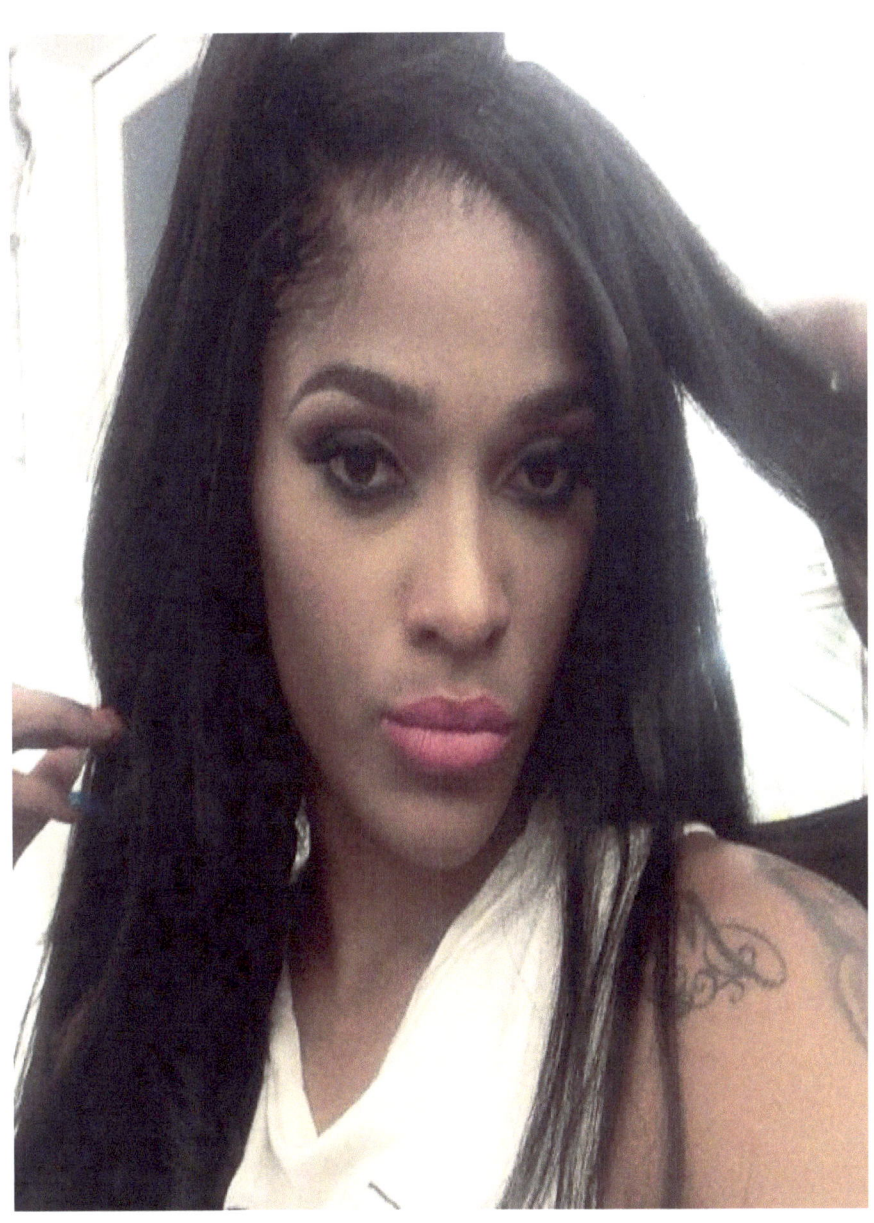

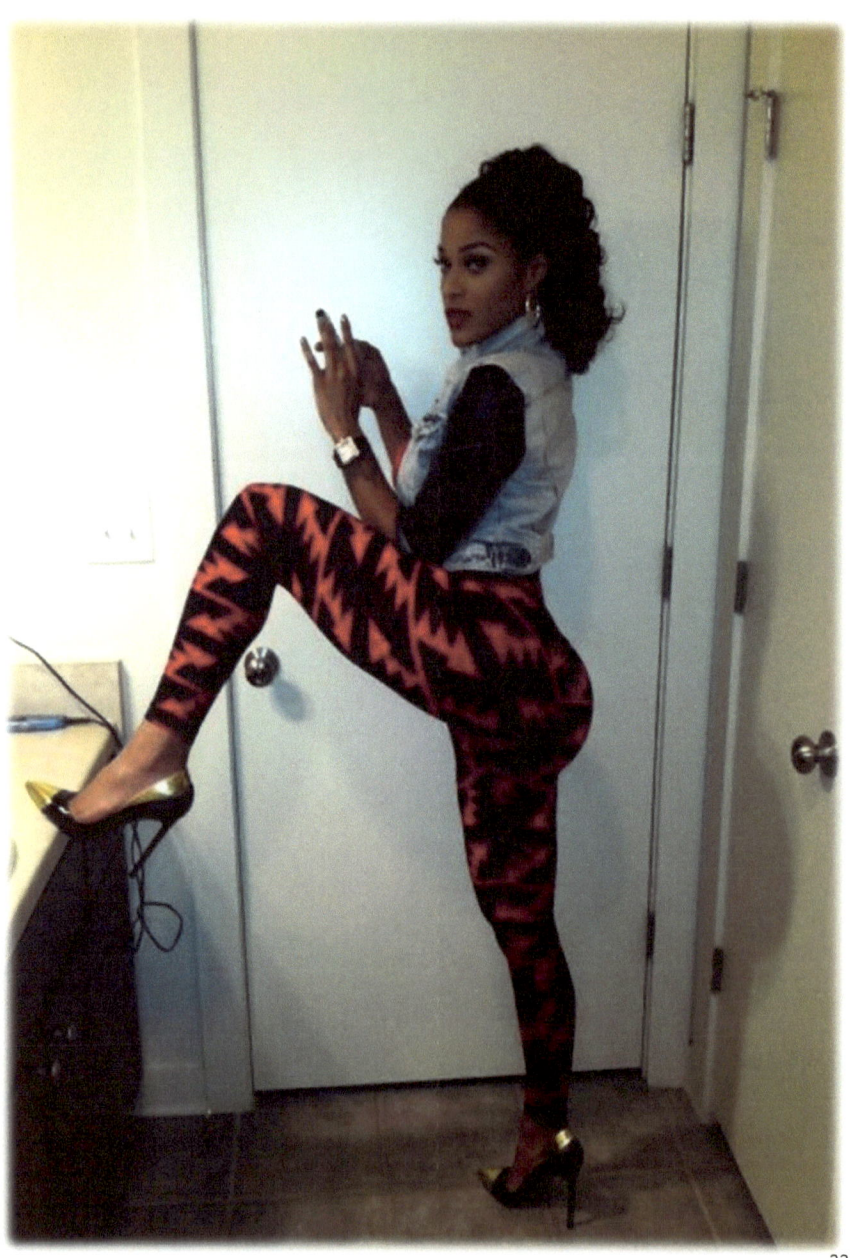

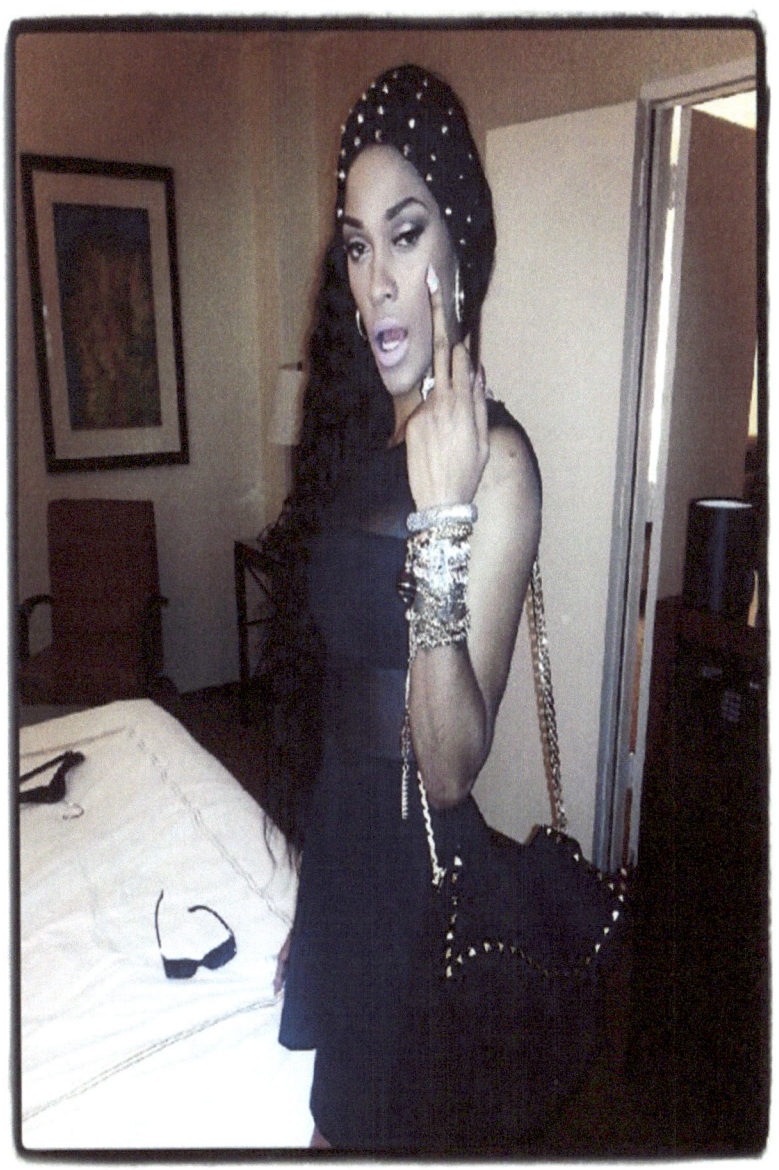

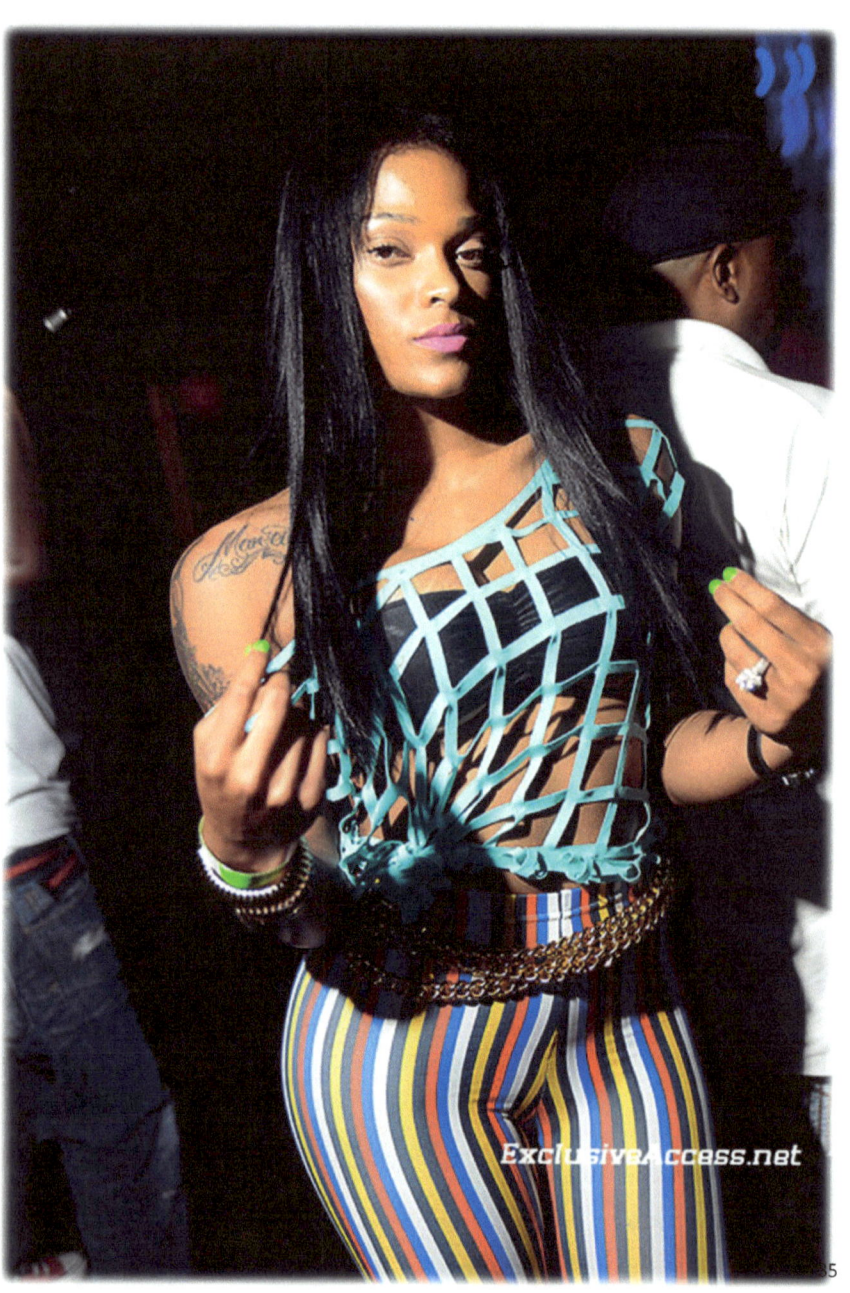

Exclusive Access.net

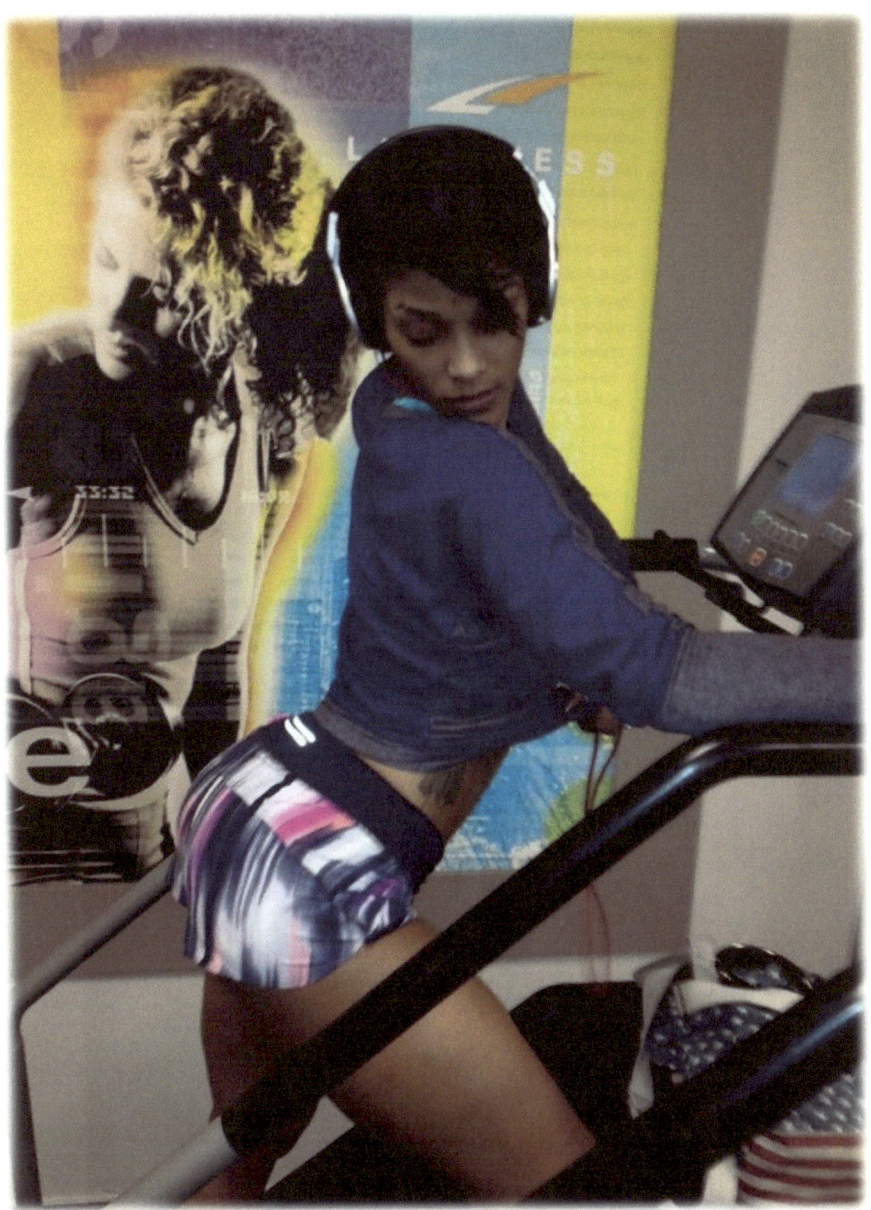

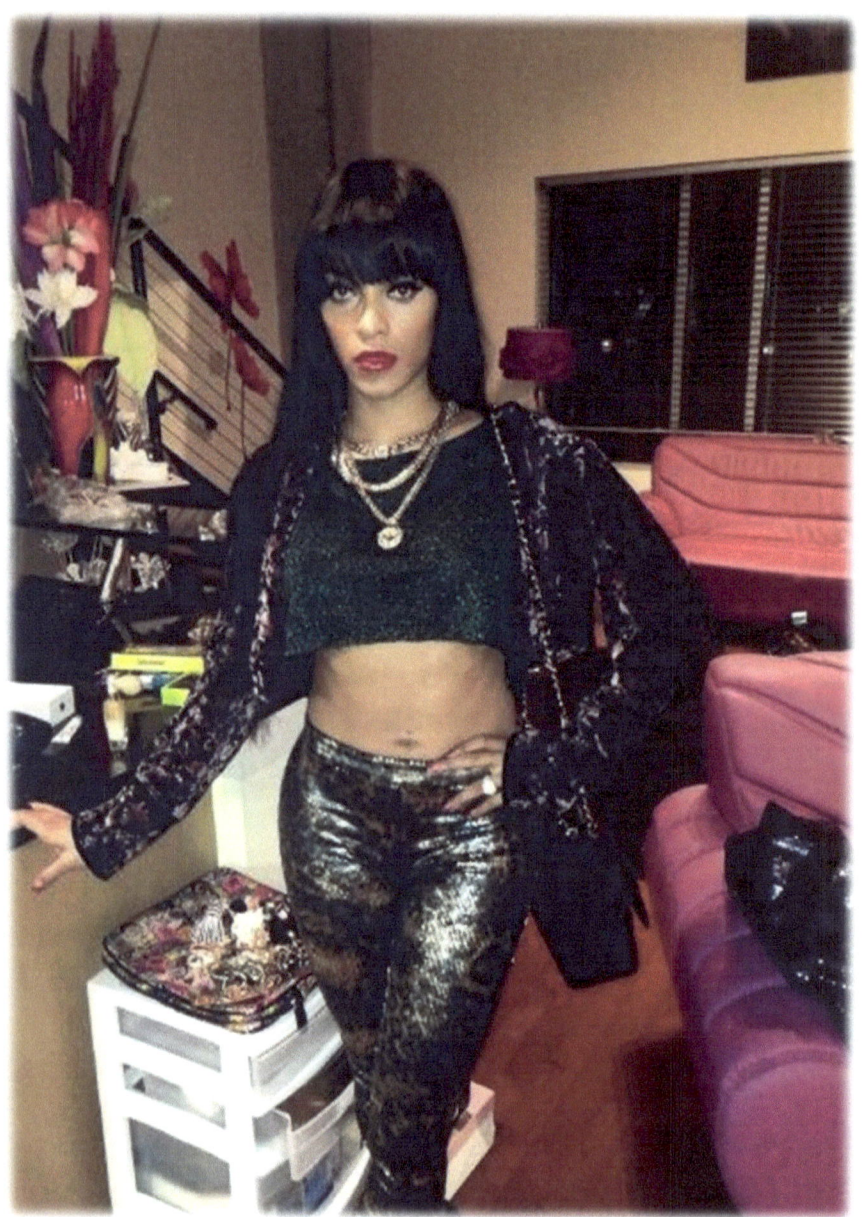

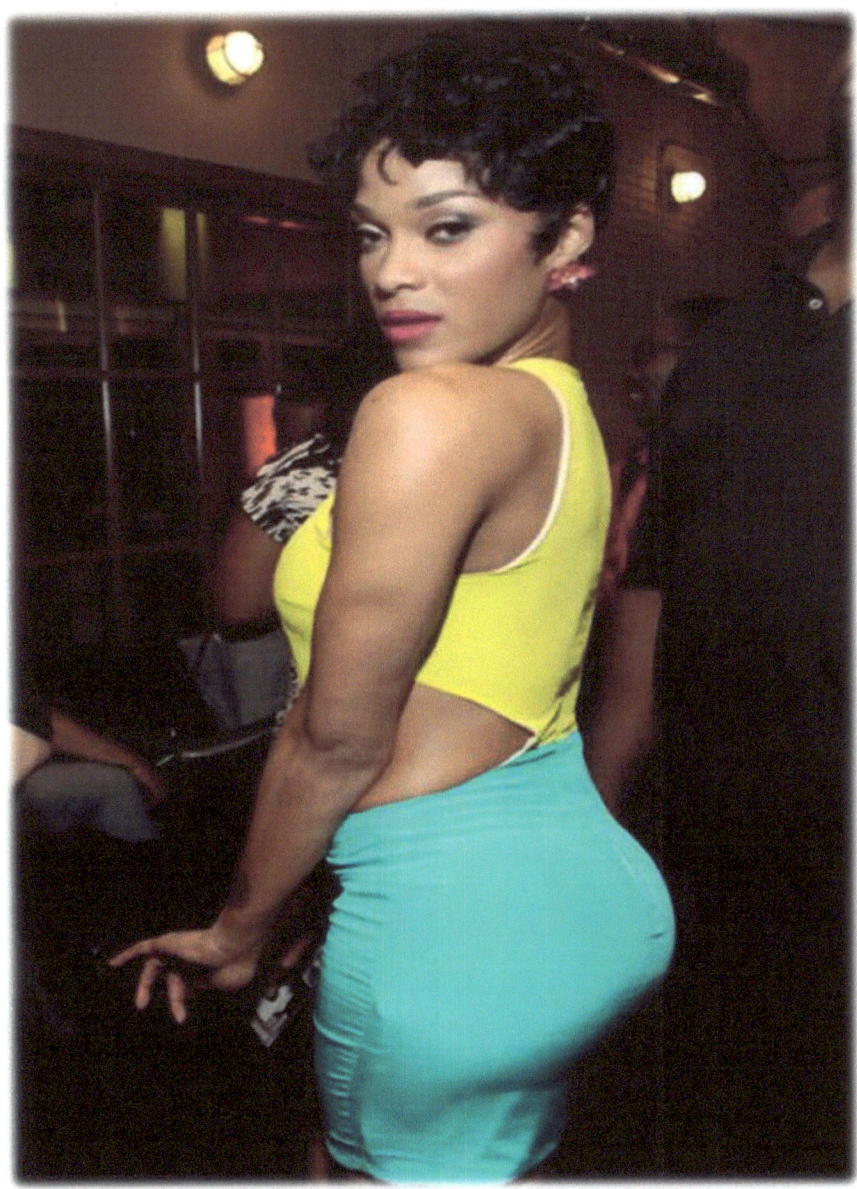

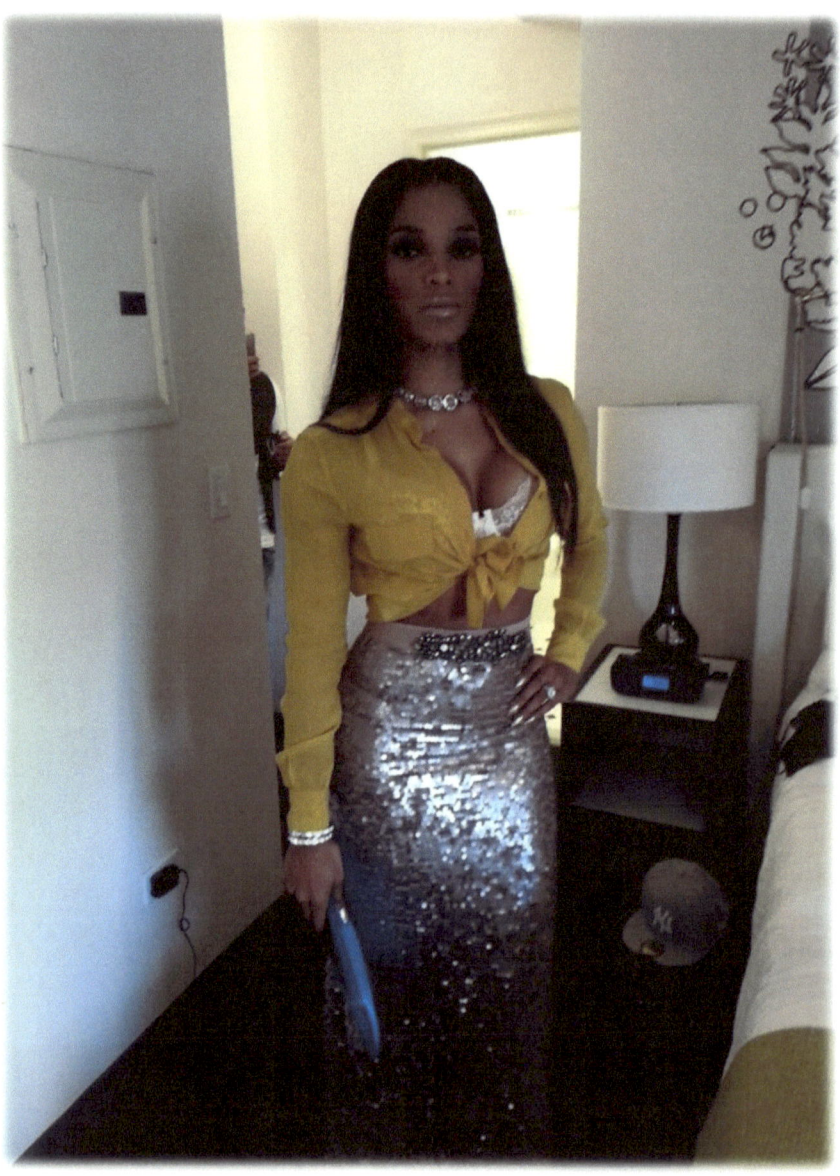

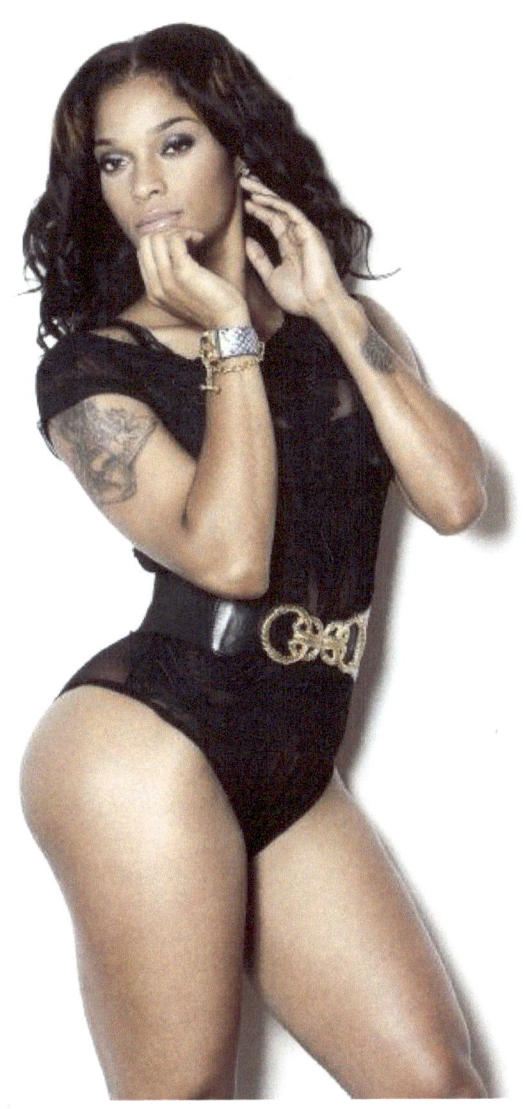

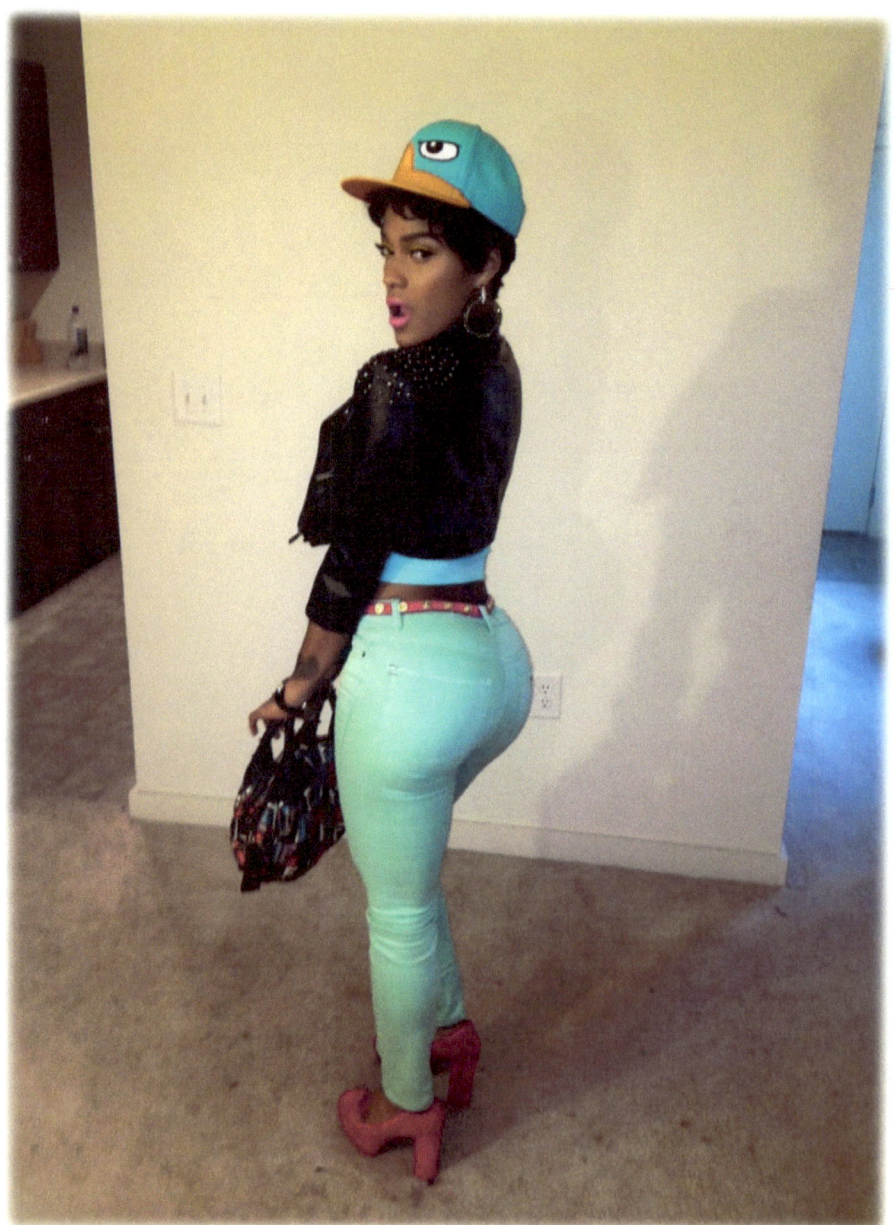

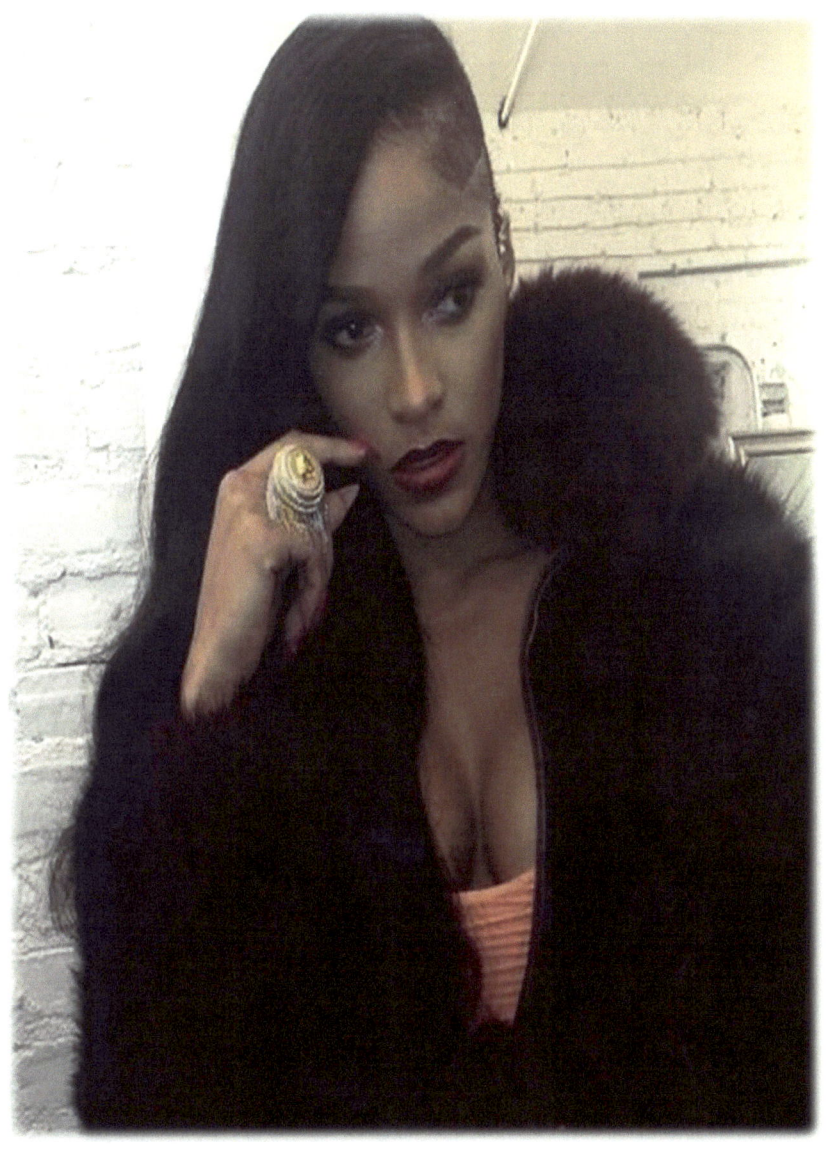

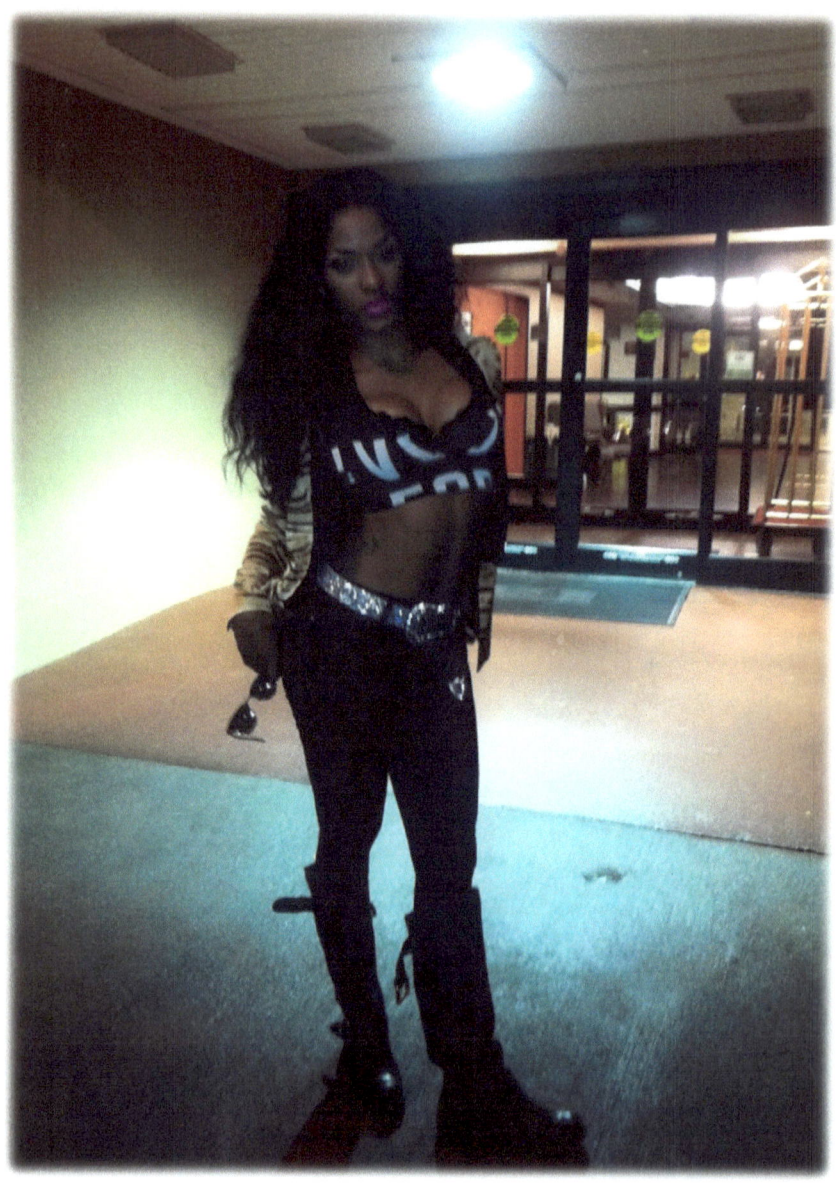

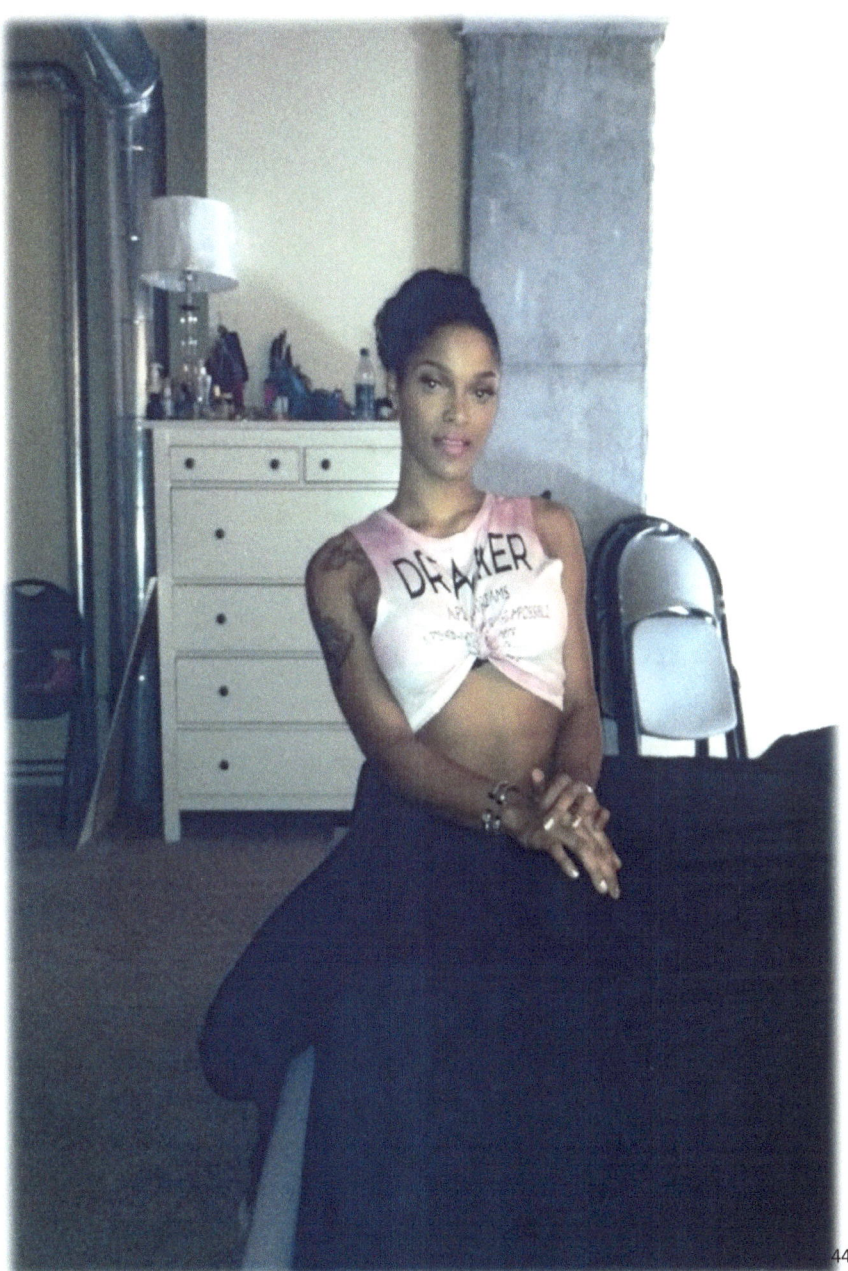

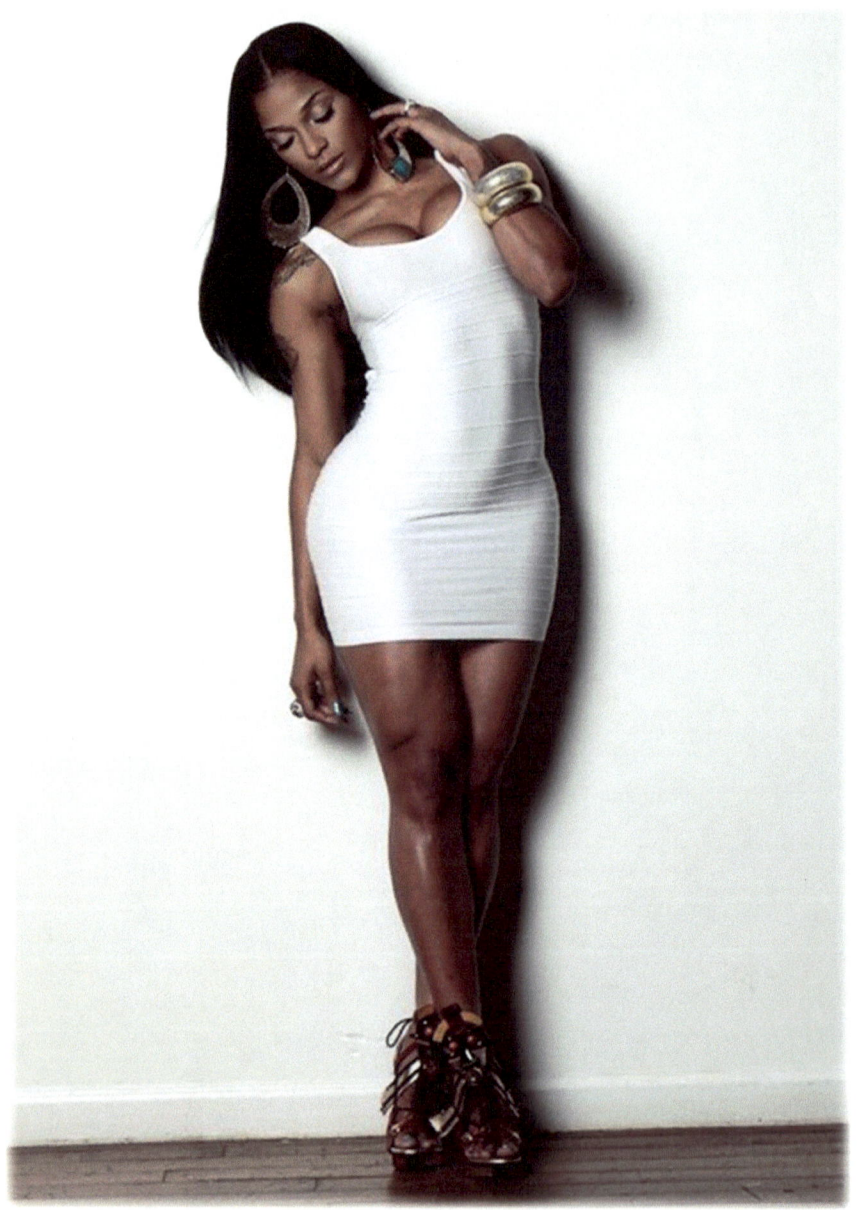

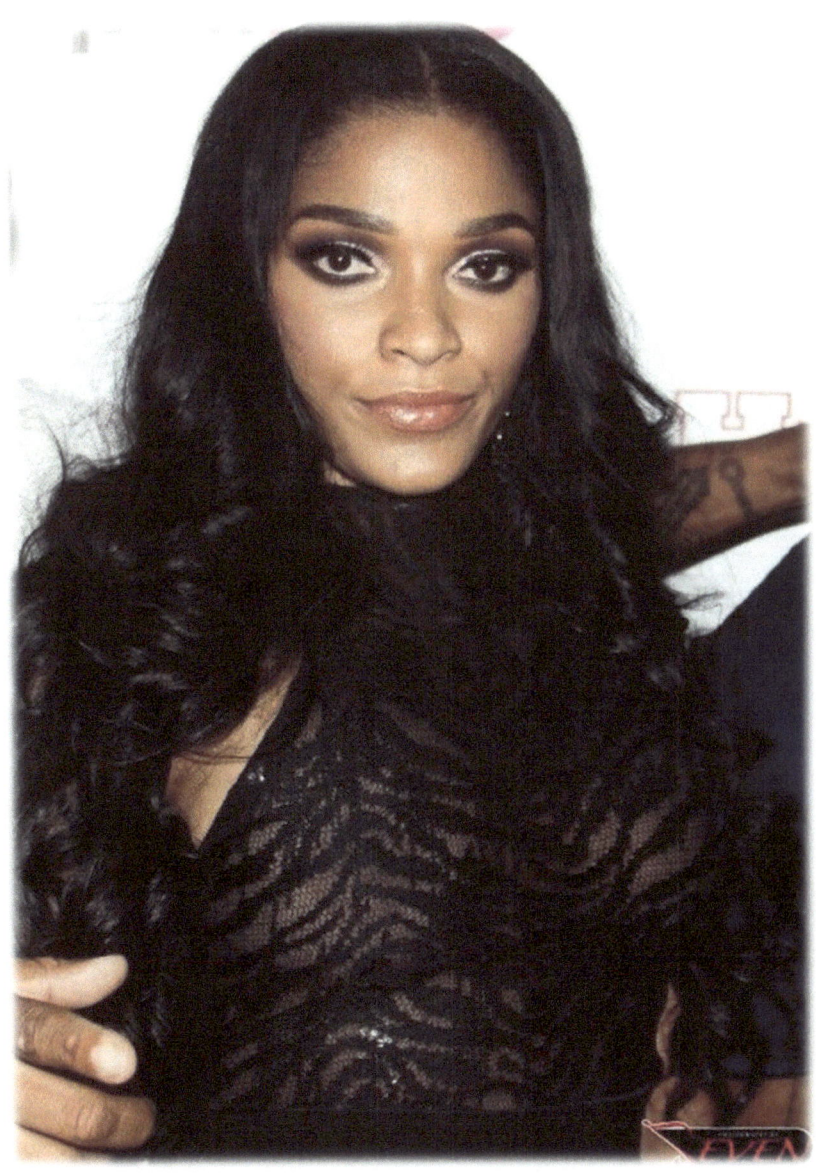

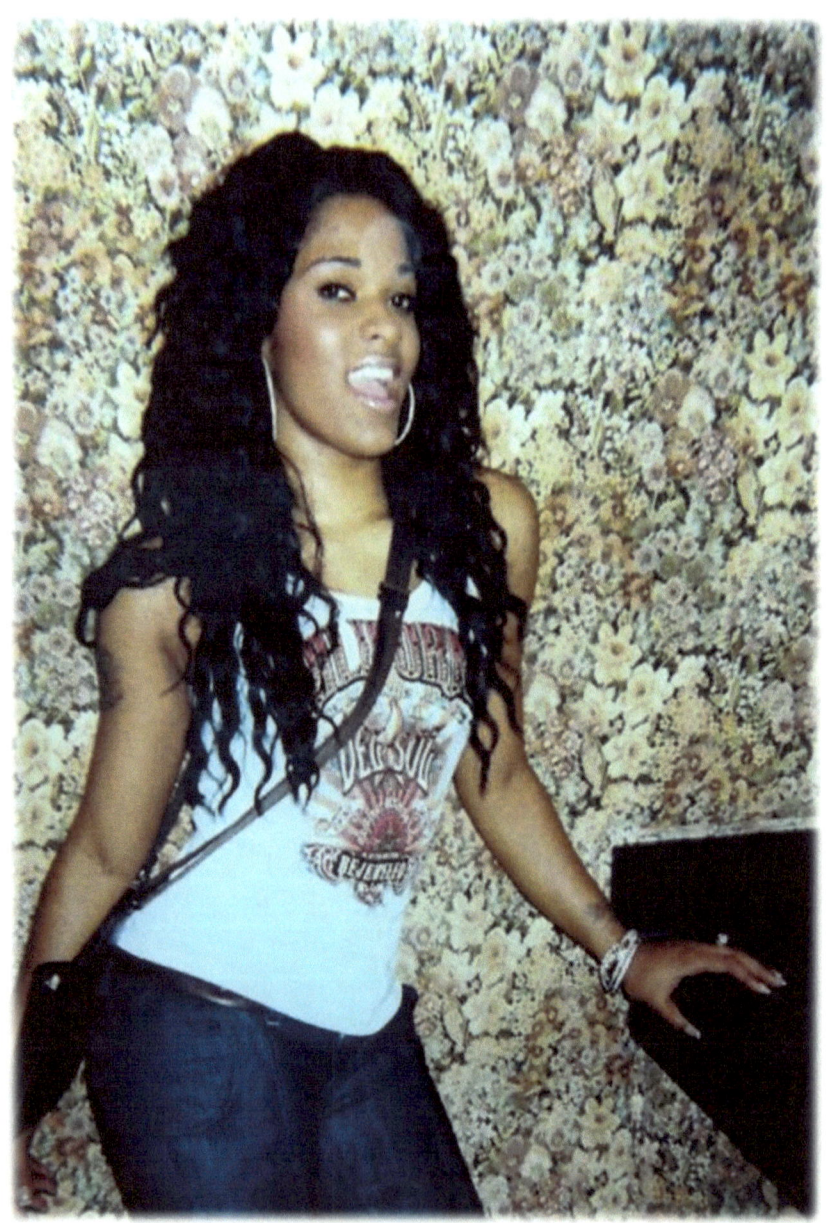

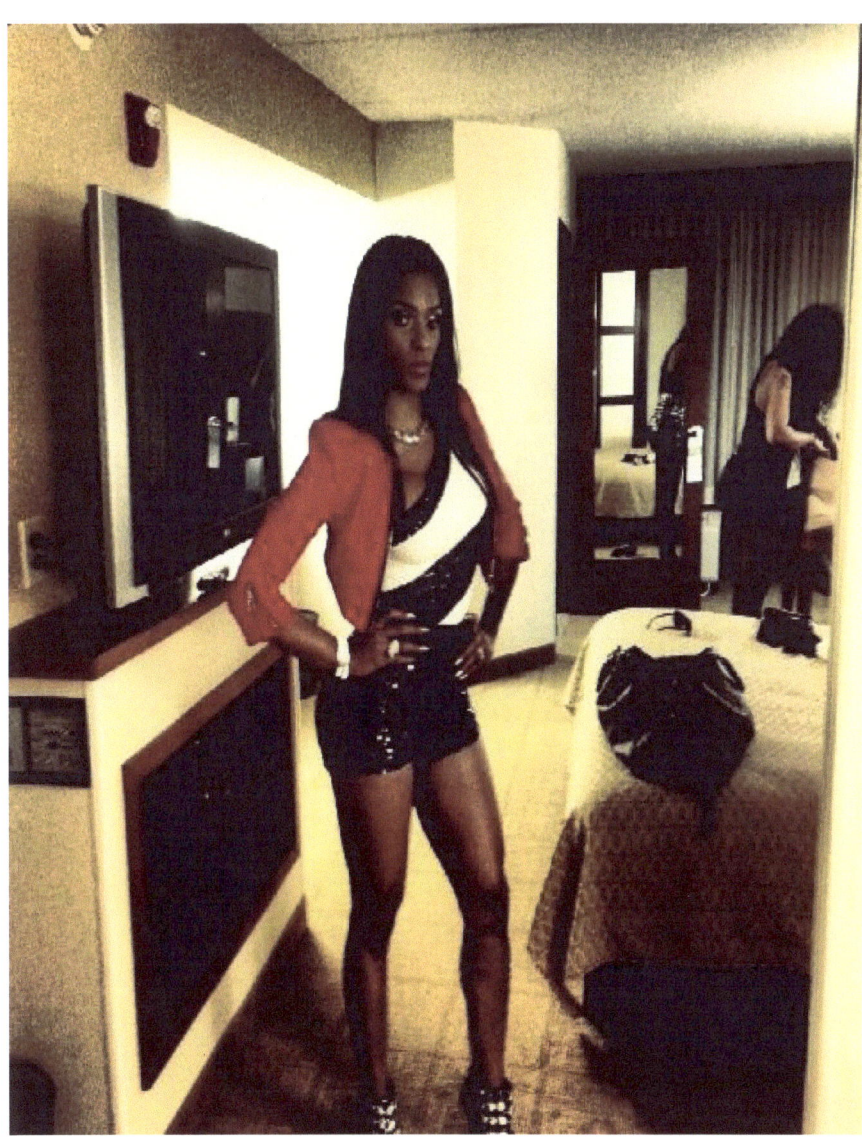

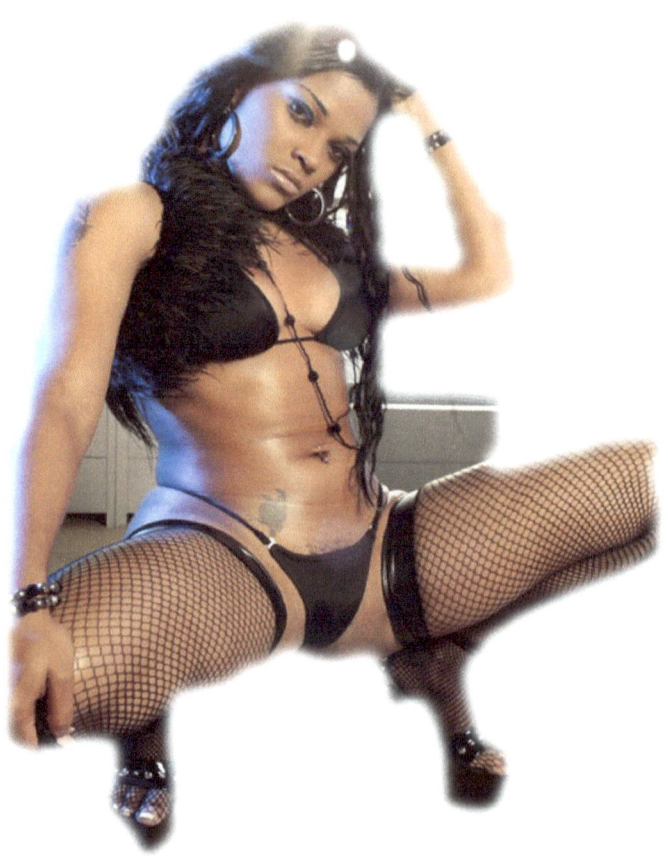

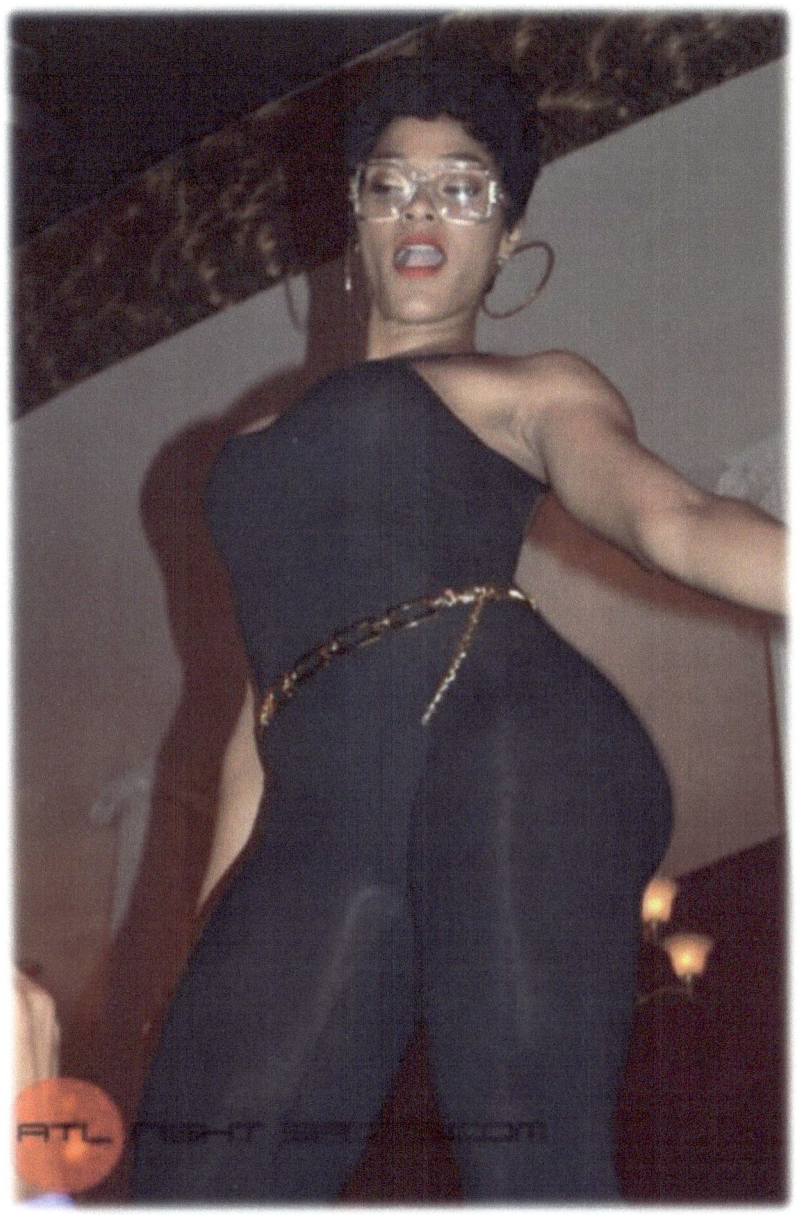

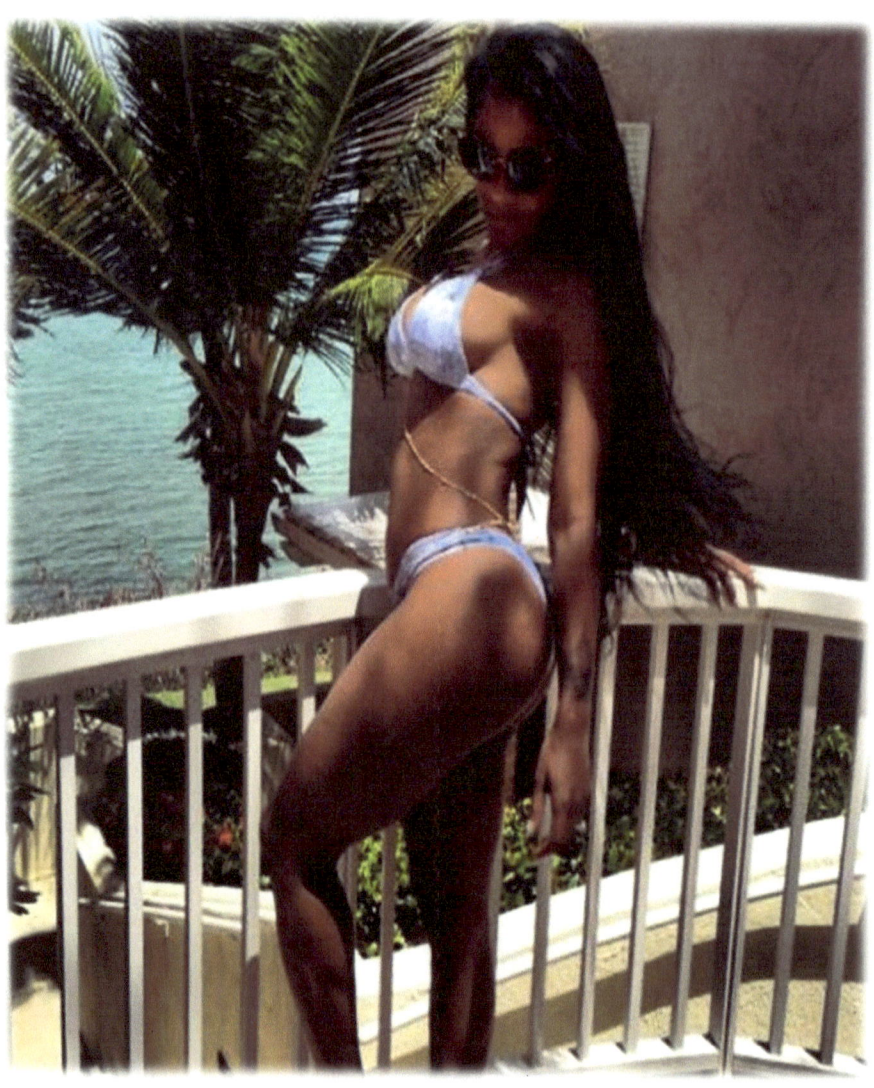

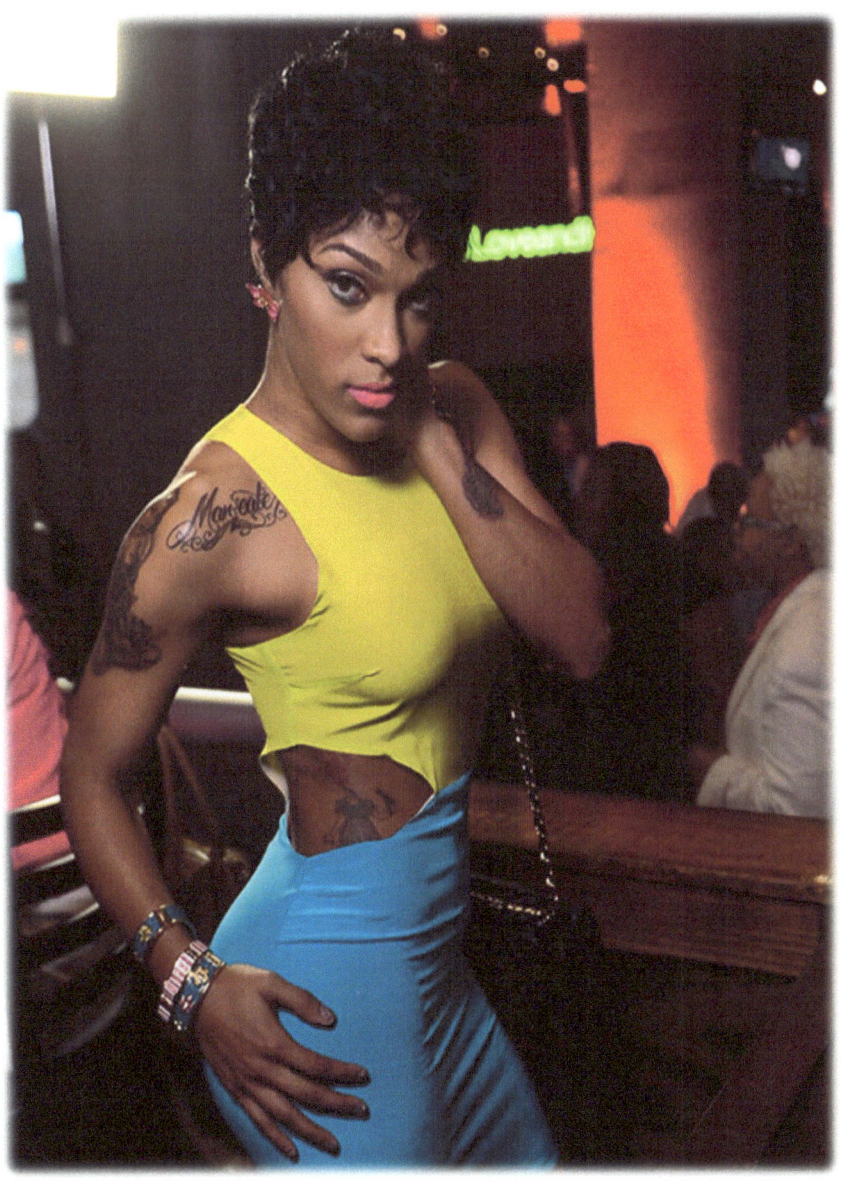

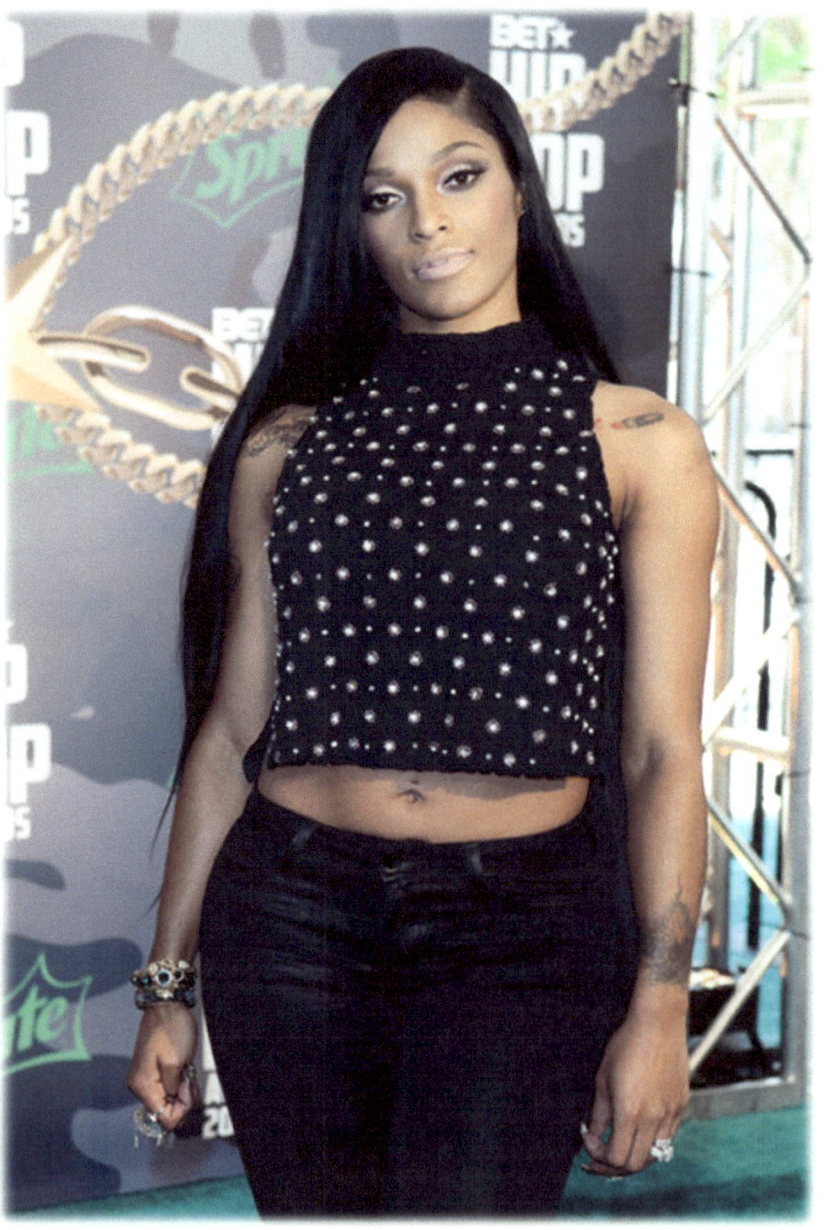

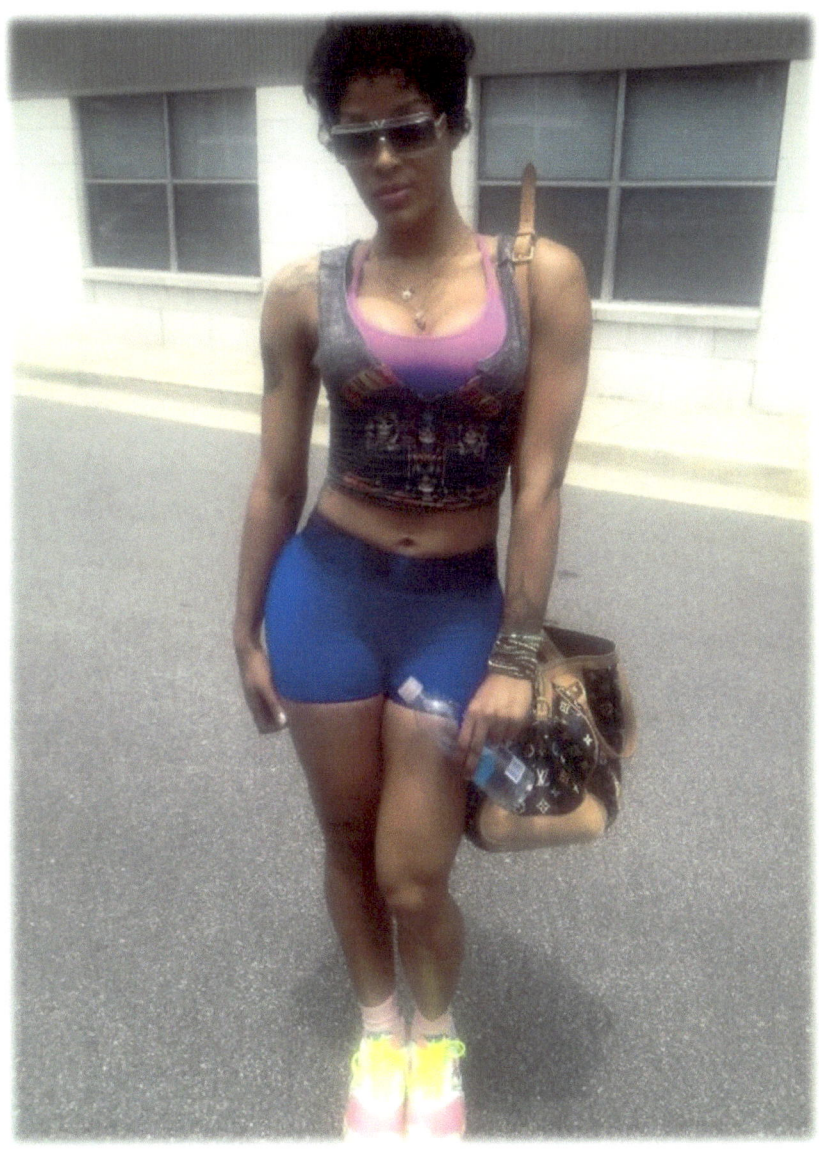

www.ingramcontent.com/pod-product-compliance
Lightning Source LLC
Chambersburg PA
CBHW040900180526
45159CB00001B/475